More Praise for Chic Thompson
and *What a Great Idea!*

"I am very impressed with Chic Thompson's idea generation techniques. I hope *What a Great Idea!* becomes a bestselling book in Japan."

> Dr. Yoshiro NakaMats
> Inventor of floppy disk, CD, and digital watch

"Coach Thompson has a delightful way of getting inside your head and playing handball with your creative juices. Heed his advice. Your creative game will improve and it will be a lot more fun to play."

> Marsh Fisher
> Founder/Chairman, Fisher Idea Systems
> Cofounder, Century 21 International

"*What a Great Idea!* is a breeding ground for new ideas!"

> Charles Prather, Ph.D.
> DuPont researcher

"Chic has a knack for getting people to see ideas that have been staring them in the face."

> Robert J. Rotella, Ph.D.
> Sports psychologist to professional athletes

"Chic opens up concepts that have been covered over by our structured way of managing."

"Chic is one of the great motivational speakers of today. His superb platform presence reaches everyone."

"If you think you are close to using all of your intellectual talent, think again. If you need to produce more original thinking in a world too captured by its habits—risk introducing your staff to this means of becoming an idea factory. I have watched Chic Thompson develop and test his methods of challenging the way executives think. It works!"

"*What a Great Idea!* can be a dangerous book in your competitors' hands. Read it before they do."

WHAT A GREAT IDEA!

WHAT A GREAT IDEA!

The Key Steps
Creative People Take

Charles "Chic" Thompson

HarperPerennial
A Division of HarperCollins*Publishers*

FIRST EDITION

Designed by Ralph Sachs

Library of Congress Cataloging-in-Publication Data

Thompson, Charles, 1948–
    What a great idea! : the key steps creative people take / Charles "Chic" Thompson. — 1st ed.
      p.   cm.
    Includes bibliographical references.
    ISBN 0-06-055317-0 (hardcover) — ISBN 0-06-096901-6 (pbk.)
    1. Creative ability. I. Title.
BF408.T46 1992
153.3'5—dc20   91-50522

92 93 94 95 96 CMG/RRD 10 9 8 7 6 5 4 3 2 1

92 93 94 95 96 CMG/RRD 10 9 8 7 6 5 4 3 2 1 (pbk.)

To my first employer, Bill Gore, who challenged me to come up with a new use for Gore-Tex every week.

To my childhood neighbor, Rube Goldberg, whose cartoons made me see solutions from a different point of view.

And, most important, to my parents, Larry and Eleanor Thompson, who supported my every act, creative and otherwise, with unconditional love.

Acknowledgments

What a Great Idea! emerged from a series of creative collaborations. First of these was my writing partnership with C. Edward Good. Ed, a consultant for law firms and corporations in the area of persuasive writing, reviewed my creativity consulting and workshop materials, scoured my notes, picked my brains, and systematically turned it all into a manuscript.

William Van Doren then edited our work, contributing additional material in many key passages and gracefully guiding the book toward finished form. Ralph Sachs meanwhile created a superb prototype for the design of this book.

Then there are the creative people who brought this work to light: Susan Moldow, my editor at HarperCollins, whose thoughtful appraisal gave me the opportunity to refine the manuscript until it met my own highest hopes for what the book would be; Rafe Sagalyn, my literary agent, who understood the value of this project and communicated it so well to HarperCollins; Bob Rotella, Tom MacAvoy, and Yoshiro NakaMats, who have each given me insight and inspiration; Victoria Dunham, Steffi Marshall, Brad King, Lee Morgan, and Berkley Ingram, my staff at Creative Management Group; Floyd Hurt and Joel Smith of Probe, Inc.; Amy Lemley and Jonathan Coleman, who guided me to Rafe; my brother Larry Thompson and Kathy Kinter; Margaret Good; Kathleen Phelan; Nancy and Joe McMoneagle; Maryellen Visconti; Kristina Myren Sheldon; and Don Borwhat, Jim Clawson, Ed Cusick, Eileen Dinan, Marsh Fisher, John Guy, Russ Linden, Captain John Miller, George Owens, John and Jacquie Pickering, Donna Sanford, John Schwab, Jerry Strand, Sharon Stromberg, and Bryce Young—friends and colleagues who made valuable suggestions after reading the initial manuscript.

Contents

ONE CREATIVE GENIUS
Yoshiro NakaMats

Dr. Yoshiro NakaMats holds more than 2,300 patents, more than double the 1,093 held by Thomas Edison. The next closest competitor holds just 400. For the past seven straight years, Dr. NakaMats has won the grand prize at the International Exposition of Inventors in New York City.

Dr. NakaMats invented the floppy disk and licensed the technology to IBM. "Does he get a royalty on the millions of disks sold every year?" I wondered; I discovered later that he does.

Among his many inventions are the compact disc, the compact disc player, the digital watch, a unique golf putter, and a water-powered engine.

When I began work on What a Great Idea! *in the early part of 1990, it occurred to me that a way to begin might be to find the "most creative person in the world" and interview him or her.*

Soon afterward, I read an intriguing article in Success *magazine about Dr. NakaMats.*

I picked up the phone and called Success. *The people there graciously provided me with Dr. NakaMats's business phone number. Checking the differences in time zones, I then waited until the appropriate Tokyo time and placed my overseas call. A receptionist answered. I explained my desire to talk with Dr. NakaMats, fully expecting to be put off. To my great surprise, the receptionist simply put me on hold, and in a very brief moment, Dr. NakaMats answered the phone.*

I was impressed and put at ease by his immediacy and openness. The first thing out of his mouth, after saying hello, was "What's your fax number?" In this preliminary, long-distance meeting, I described my company—Creative Management Group—my creativity workshops, and my plans for this book. We agreed to share information immediately through our respective fax machines.

Within a few days after my initial call, Dr. NakaMats called back and said he would be in Pittsburgh in April to unveil his latest invention. Pittsburgh provided another lure, however. An avid baseball fan and former collegiate pitcher, Dr. NakaMats had been invited to throw out the first ball for the Pittsburgh Pirates' opening game. I immediately requested, and felt very fortunate to receive, an interview.

When we met in Pittsburgh, I was struck by the man's balance: he was formal when he needed to be formal, but he also knew how to be comfortable. In fact, when I first met him, he had just bought his first pair of Dock-Siders and began asking me all about American clothing. On reflection I found it very significant that the idea man wasn't so much telling me things as asking me questions.

What began as a half-hour interview turned into one of the most memorable experiences of my life: a five-hour conversation with the most creative inventor on the globe today! Graciously, he permitted me to include highlights of that interview here.

We sat side by side in stuffed chairs in the dimly lighted, luxurious "trophy room" of an old private club—the Duquesne Club, in Pittsburgh, Pennsylvania. In the large, walnut-paneled space, decorated in richly hued fabrics, it was just he (the inventor), I (the writer), and his wife (the recorder, who got part of the interview on camcorder).

I'd seen his picture in newspapers and magazines, but still he was much younger looking than I expected. Most striking was his combination of youthful enthusiasm and attentive wisdom.

IN MY COUNTRY, THE DRIVE TO SUCCEED—and the competition— is unbelievably intense. From early on, Japanese children are under enormous pressure to learn. I was fortunate that my parents encouraged my natural curiosity along with my academic learning from the very beginning. They gave me the freedom to create and invent—which I've been doing for as long as I can remember.

What are the teaching methods used to prepare Japanese children for the strong competition they face? And how does this affect creativity?

One method is memorization. We teach our kids to memorize until the age of twenty, for we have discovered that the human brain needs memorization up to that point. Then young people can begin free-associating, putting everything together. That's how geniuses are formed.

If a child doesn't learn how to memorize effectively, he doesn't reach his full potential.

So you feel that creativity comes from a balance of regimentation and freedom?

Yes, but freedom is most important of all. Genius lies in developing complete and perfect freedom within a human being. Only then can a person come up with the best ideas.

We have a difficult time in this country because we don't allow ourselves that kind of freedom. We have what we call the Protestant work ethic that says, "If at first you don't succeed, try and try again." To me, trying too hard stifles creativity.

That's unfortunate. It's crucial to be able to find the time and the freedom to develop your best ideas.

Then tell me about your routine to spark creativity. I've heard that you come up with ideas underwater!

Yes, that's part of a three-step process. When developing ideas, the first rule is *You have to be calm*. So I've created what I call my "static" room. It's a place of peace and quiet. In this room, I only have natural things: a rock garden, natural running water, plants, a five-ton boulder from Kyoto. The walls are white. I can look out on the Tokyo skyline, but in the room there is no metal or concrete—only natural things like water and rock and wood.

So you go into your "static" room to meditate?

No, just the opposite! I go into the room to free-associate. It's what you must do *before* meditating, *before* focusing on one thing. I just throw out ideas—I let my mind wander where it will.

I call that "naive incubation."

Yes, it's my time to let my mind be free. Then I go into my "dynamic" room, which is just the opposite of my "static" room. The "dynamic" room is dark, with black-and-white-striped walls, leather furniture, and special audio and video equipment. I've created speakers with frequencies between 12 and 40,000 hertz—which, you can imagine, are quite powerful. I start out listening to jazz, then change to what you call "easy listening," and always end with Beethoven's Fifth Symphony. For me, Beethoven's Fifth is good music for conclusions.

> "I have a special way of holding my breath and swimming underwater— that's when I come up with my best ideas."

And finally you go to your swimming pool . . .

Exactly—the final stage. I have a special way of holding my breath and swimming underwater—that's when I come up with my best ideas. I've created a Plexiglas writing pad so that I can stay underwater and record these ideas. I call it "creative swimming."

That seems to fit very well with the strategy I teach in my creativity workshops: discover and use your "idea-friendly times."

Yes, but in doing this, you must prepare your body. You can only eat the best foods. You cannot drink alcohol.

I've heard that you've come up with your own "brain food."

Yes, these are snacks I've invented, which I eat during the day. I've marketed them as Yummy Nutri Brain Food. They are very helpful to the brain's thinking process. They are a special mixture of dried shrimp, seaweed, cheese, yogurt, eel, eggs, beef, and chicken livers—all fortified with vitamins.

How many people—technicians, researchers, and assistants—do you employ to help with your inventions?

In all, I have 110 employees.

And what exactly do they do?

They work with my ideas, make prototypes, and give other assistance with details.

Do you come up with ideas at night?

I come up with ideas anytime! I only sleep four hours a night.

That's interesting—that's very similar to Thomas Edison. Do you take naps like he did?

Yes. Twice a day I take thirty-minute naps in a special chair I've designed—the Cerebrex chair. It improves memory, math skills, and creativity, and it can lower blood pressure, improve eyesight, and cure other ailments.

How does the Cerebrex work?

Special sound frequencies pulse from footrest to headrest, stimulating blood circulation and increasing synaptic activity in the brain. An hour in my chair refreshes the brain as much as eight hours of sleep.

So, like Edison, you're awake most of the time. Do you agree with Edison's claim that ideas are 1 percent inspiration and 99 percent perspiration?

No, now it's just the opposite! Now it's 1 percent perspiration and 99 percent "ikispiration." Now, more than ever, we have to have ikispiration. This means I encourage myself to go through my three elements of creation: *suji*, the theory of knowledge; *pika*, inspiration; and *iki*, practicality, feasibility, and marketability. In order to be successful, you must go through all three stages and make sure that your ideas stand up to all of them, which is ikispiration. Also, these days, the computer saves time and cuts out the 99 percent perspiration.

Do you find that most American research-and-development firms take themselves through your three stages?

Most are very thorough with *suji*, or theory, but don't concentrate on the *iki*, marketability. Hardest of all, of course, is *pika*, the creative inspiration. Researchers often have trouble with *pika* because they're too focused on one particular element. A genius must be a well-rounded person, familiar with many things: art, music, science, sports. He or she can't be restricted to only one field of expertise.

> *"Now it's 1 percent perspiration and 99 percent 'ikispiration.'"*

Well, you certainly appear to practice what you preach. You know so much about music, about art, about sports . . .

That's what genius is, when you're able to discuss, and to be good at, many things. As much as I enjoy hearing about the things you [Chic] have invented during your chemistry career, about your teaching, about your video programs, I'm most fascinated by the fact that a person who can be a chemist and a teacher and a speaker can also be a cartoonist. And at such a young age!

Well, people do kid me about looking young, but I could say the same thing about you.

That comes from eating the right foods and participating in the right athletics. Certain activities I believe aren't good for creativity. To be creative, you must have perfect freedom. Sports like jogging, tennis, and golf, I don't believe, are conducive to the brain waves for creativity.

> "I'd like to see the work ethic in the U.S. more geared to creativity."

Hmmmm. I'd really like to see your research on that, because I know a lot of people who feel they come up with their ideas when they go out jogging. Maybe, for Americans, because we don't allow ourselves to have perfect freedom at work, we can get part of the way there by jogging or golfing—that's the only time we give ourselves permission to be free enough to come up with new ideas.

Maybe so, but they won't be your *best* ideas—you're not at your peak creative performance if you have to use athletics or techniques to get your ideas. It's only when you have perfect freedom that your best ideas come out.

What are some of your suggestions to American executives on ways to become more creative?

I'd like to see the work ethic in the United States more geared to creativity. We need more creative people and more creative leaders. Governments as a whole *must* learn to be more creative. I've just written a book called *The Invention of Government*. I'm trying to show that through the creative process, governments—not just individuals—can be more innovative. Among my goals right now are working in political reform in Japan and improving our relationship with the United States. I want Americans and others to understand that many of the perceived barriers between nations—trade barriers, cultural barriers—aren't as strong as people think they are. It's just that we don't understand each other as well as we should, and that means we must become more open with each other.

> "Through the creative process, governments—not just individuals—can be more innovative."

In that regard, I'm very impressed by your openness to discuss and to spend so many hours with me. So many people in the United States who have one or two good ideas don't share them with anyone. They're afraid that people are going to steal them. And here you've opened up an International Genius Convention—for everyone to display their ideas.

My rationale is very simple: we *need* to open up the world. We *need* to share and to interact. I always tell young inventors to forget about money as a primary motivator and to concentrate on ideas that will benefit mankind. If you do this, the money will automatically follow! And, by inventions, I don't just mean visible items. There are invisible inventions, too.

> *"An 'invisible' invention is . . . a new way of teaching something, a new way to spark creativity in others. 'Invisible' inventions are just as powerful and far-reaching —if not more so— than 'visible' inventions."*

"Invisible" inventions?

An "invisible" invention is something you can't see but can use. It's a new way of teaching something, a new way to spark creativity in others. "Invisible" inventions are just as powerful and far-reaching—if not more so—than "visible" inventions.

You're 62 now. Are you becoming more creative every day?

Of course. Because I always strive to be better. You must use your life! If you have a power of 10 and only use an 8, that is not satisfaction. If you have a power of 10 and use a 12, *that* is satisfaction. I will always follow my three elements of invention, which I recommend to everyone, not just to inventors. *Suji*, *pika*, and *iki* can be used by executives in any company or organization—they simply apply these principles to their own particular challenges. As for continuing the creative process as a person gets older, well, at 62, I feel that I'm still relatively young. Many scientists believe that we can live to be 120. I believe, through my formulas, that we can live to be 144. I'm spending a lot of my time studying longevity.

I'm working with some physicians here in the United States who are interested in maximizing the life span and in improving the quality of life. I'll line it up so you can talk with them.

Excellent! I'll make time. I'm very interested.

I've read that you come up with a patentable idea every day. Have you come up with one today?

No, so let's invent a product together. What would you buy today if it were available?

I'd buy a recording device, about the size of a credit card, that could fit in my shirt pocket. Every time I had a flash of an idea, I could just record it. It would be voice-activated, with a very large memory, and have a voice-activated filing system for idea management.

What would you call it?

I'd call it "Flash"— because it would just be flashes of ideas, which you could then download onto a computer system.

Very good. *[He then gave me a ten-minute education on microtechnology and a grilling on what I thought of the idea's market potential.]* This will be our first product together, so when I get home, I'll turn it over to my research department.

Let me thank you. You seem to have the ability to network and to learn from others all the time.

That's what it takes to succeed. And, for every meeting, I like to keep a visual record. That's why my wife has been taking pictures and recording our conversation on the camcorder. When something is on video, I can go back and reference the face and the voice, not just written notes. Now, would you please type in your name?

Excuse me?

Type in your name on this infrared recorder, and it will appear directly on the photographs that we took, along with today's date.

I've never seen anything like this!

I know. One of my recent inventions.

This interview was recorded April 29, 1990, in Pittsburgh, Pennsylvania, at the Duquesne Club.

CREATIVITY TODAY
The Innovation Mind-Set

*We need to make the world safe for creativity and intuition,
for it's creativity and intuition that will make the world safe
for us.*

> —*Edgar Mitchell,* Apollo *Astronaut*

Most of us are not naturally born innovators or visionaries. Indeed, by nature, most people resist change and innovation. For example, in 1899, the nation's steward of innovation—the director of the U.S. Patent Office—said that "everything that can be invented has been invented." He then proceeded to request that the Patent Office be dismantled and that he be transferred to a new position in government.

To foster change and creativity, to establish an organization where, quoting Jack Welch, CEO of General Electric, "people have the freedom to be creative, a place that brings out the best in everybody," we need to make idea generation and idea implementation firmly ingrained habits. A mind-set, if you will. To produce this idea-friendly frame of mind, we need to understand and honor the creative processes routinely employed by the world's most creative inventors, thinkers, writers, leaders, and artists.

It seems we've always known the power of ideas. A mark of our century, however, may be that we've tended to try to generate ideas through programs. We've studied and followed the newest theories of management from Japan. We've bought books on excellence, handed them out to all managers, visited them once a week, and thought we were managing by walking around. We've bought books on ancient military strategists, given them to all managers, and expected them to band together, draw their swords, and charge. We've even purchased books on managing in sixty seconds flat, delivered them to all managers along with a helpful memo encouraging them to read and heed.

It's not that we haven't benefited a great deal from most of these programs; we have. But one of their functions has been to help us recognize that we still need to tap and protect the source of great ideas. For truly great ideas will not flourish in organizations top-heavy with programs. Great ideas grow in organizations with a vision, a mind-set devoted to innovation and continuous improvement—to finding a better way every day. And this outlook must acknowledge the primacy of the individual imagination—of creative freedom.

As a teacher of creativity to audiences around the world, I have had the opportunity to interview and survey more than ten thousand senior executives and researchers in private and public organizations. My work has consisted largely of helping creative people gain access to universal ways of discovering and developing new ideas. In this book, you'll learn proven, flexible techniques that can help you or your organization generate ideas immediately. At the same time, you will probably become empowered to make creativity a more conscious and powerful part of your life and work.

You're already abundantly creative. The techniques that follow can allow you greater freedom to understand, access, enjoy, and use that creativity.

By cultivating our creative freedom, we can all join more fully in the underlying movement of this decade and the coming century. We begin, as we will end, with recognition of the free human spirit, one of the greatest of the world's truly great ideas.

CHIC THOMPSON
Charlottesville, Virginia
January 1992

The First Step

FREEDOM

The first step creative people take, whether or not they do it consciously, is to gain the inner freedom to consider new ideas and new possibilities. This step isn't always as easy as it sounds.

Many of us have incorporated within ourselves obstacles and barricades to the consideration of new horizons, particularly when these new vistas involve our own thoughts, our own dreams—our own potentially great ideas. Most of us need help to break the bonds we've placed around our own creativity.

Chapter 1

A TEASPOON OF BAKING SODA
The Nature of Creativity

Add one teaspoon of baking soda for each batch of two dozen cookies . . .

One teaspoon, for heaven's sake. For two dozen cookies. Not a cup. Not a half cup. Not even a tablespoon. What a business to be in! Selling baking soda by the teaspoon. Not much future there. The box would just sit around on the shelf, next to the spices, until it . . . until it . . . until it begins to smell like oregano?

Hey, the stuff absorbs odors!

And where in our lives could we use a little of this odor-absorbing ability of baking soda?

Car ashtrays . . .

Running shoes . . .

The cat's litter box . . .

Underarms . . .

The refrigerator . . .

The refrigerator! Baking soda in a refrigerator. The whole box, folks. Not just one measly teaspoon. Imagine what that great idea did to the sales of baking soda at Arm & Hammer.

From one teaspoon to the whole box. No, make that two boxes. One for the veggies and one for the ice cream. How about a box in my golf locker . . . . We're on a roll.

We've just witnessed one of the most vital principles of creativity

> **CREATIVE RULE OF THUMB #1**
>
> **The best way to get great ideas is to get lots of ideas and throw the bad ones away.**

at work: The best way to get great ideas is to get lots of ideas and throw the bad ones away.

What is creativity? How do we come up with our ideas?

What is the magic that can alter the way we use baking soda or revolutionize the way we communicate or transform our view of the world?

Creativity and the Idea Person

Although *creativity* is difficult to define, for our purposes let's put it this way:

> *Creativity is the ability to look at the same thing as everyone else but to see something different.*

Many people envy "Idea People" and marvel at the flow of ideas they seem to churn out almost without effort. Many people wish they could be more creative but feel resigned to a lesser, duller fate. Idea People, after all, were just born that way.

Fortunately, that's a myth.

Creativity is not a trait monopolized by a few fortunate souls. Every person is creative, because creativity is the trait that makes us human. *Creativity* is just another way to describe *intelligence*. To be creative is to have intelligence, to be able to gather information, and to make decisions based on that information. To be creative is to be able to perceive and recognize the world around us, to understand what we need or wish to do in response to it, and to set about changing it. To be creative is to find a way, a thought, an expression, a human manifestation no one else has found and to bring newly discovered possibilities into reality.

The Creative Process

How do we change the world? Just by coming up with great ideas? No, creativity is more than idea generation. The greatest idea on earth is worthless unless acted on. Someone must evaluate the quality of the idea. Someone must take the idea and run with it. Someone must develop the necessary systems of people, machinery, finances, packaging, distribution, service, and marketing. Those systems need ongoing management. The Idea People alone are not enough.

Creativity isn't so much a personality trait or a talent as it is a process, a continuum. From the beginning of an idea to its ultimate fruition, all along this line, a variety of people with different abilities and traits play vital roles. The Idea Generator gives birth to the idea. The Idea Promoter sees an array of applications of the idea and sets in motion the forces to try out the more promising ones. The Idea Systems Designer creates the organizations of people, machines, space, and money and gets them rolling toward the goal. The Idea Implementers establish the routine tasks necessary for reaching that goal. And all along the way Idea Evaluators constantly question the quality and effectiveness of the way things work . . . and don't work.

Contemplate the process and you'll see yourself somewhere along this line:

Generation . . .

Promotion . . .

Design . . .

Implementation . . .

Evaluation . . .

You might see your role and your traits pop up in several of these areas. Or perhaps you'll see that you primarily do best in just one. You might even see that you shy away from some of the other functions. If you're an Idea Implementer, and particularly if you don't understand your own creativity, you might resent the Evaluator, envy the Generator, and barely tolerate the Promoter. If you're an Idea Generator, you'd probably rather run naked through the snow than implement the nitty-gritty details of your own idea.

So the Idea Generator is the one most of us call "creative." The Idea Generator just has that knack of coming up with great ideas. But what about the Idea Promoter? The Designer? The Implementer? The Evaluator? Mustn't they be creative as well?

Indeed, won't each participant in this creative process be more creative by developing the characteristics of others in the process? Certainly the Implementer who takes on the characteristics of the Generator will come up with some great ideas for the implementation process. And the Generator who understands the ins and outs of implementation will become a generator of better, more workable ideas, ideas that are likely to be more efficient and more realistic.

I believe that the keys to a successful creative process are three: first, the ability to recognize that all these types of people are necessary for successful creativity; second, the ability to see yourself as you are and as other people most likely see you; and third, the ability to try other creative styles on for size. As you develop and mature, you need to see those areas in the creative process that naturally attract you and then try out skills needed by the other areas.

You can flex, and stretch, your unused creative muscles. Once you do, you'll never be the same again. In the words of Oliver Wendell Holmes:

> *The human mind once stretched to a new idea never goes back to its original dimensions.*

Your Idea Muscles

This book will help you do some mind stretching. It teaches you a method for coming up with great ideas. Ideas that are light-years ahead of their time? No. To borrow from Woody Allen, the best idea is fifteen minutes ahead of its time. Those that are light-years ahead often are ignored and certainly get delayed. The copier machine was "light-years" ahead when Chester Carlson invented it in 1929 and Xerox introduced it in 1948. It took twenty more years, until 1968, to become essential to our offices. The office fax machine was "fifteen minutes" ahead and became a standard office fixture within two years.

> **CREATIVE RULE OF THUMB #2**
>
> **Create ideas that are fifteen minutes ahead of their time . . . not light-years ahead.**

You can extend your creativity beyond your current perspective, and I can help. For I'm one of those Idea Generators. I share many of their traits. I have some of the Idea Promoter and Designer in me as well. I do have that ability to see solutions other people don't; I can come up with some great ones and some not so great ones. All my life, I've had this ability to see things differently . . . very differently.

Why? Because I have dyslexia.

I read words in a different way. I see numbers in a different way. For that reason, I shied away from the written word in school and gravitated toward the spoken word. I couldn't deal very effectively with written words so I became rather good at giving speeches. In grade school, for example, I ran for class president; when I gave my first campaign speech, my opponent bowed out of the race.

Because of this "handicap," I also gravitated toward pictorial depictions of situations, problems, and solutions to problems. I developed my artistic ability and became fairly adept at cartooning. At one time, I even worked for Walt Disney Productions. Mr. Disney was fond of saying: "It's always fun to do the impossible." I was fond of adding: "Because that's where there's less competition."

I had a falling-out with the powers at Disney when I suggested that they consider putting some of their educational cartoons on videotape for sale and rental to schools and libraries. What a great idea that was! But the president of Disney at that time said, "We will never release our cartoon films on videotape. There's too great a danger of illegal copying." That same year, Disney sued Sony over the introduction of the Betamax videotape recorder.

So I took my "impossible" idea and started my own company, Creative Media Group, Inc. That company developed some rather successful cartoon videos in the health field. My firm, for example, was the first on the market with a video about the dangers of AIDS.

Our video *AIDS Alert* is now translated into more than eleven languages and was recently captioned for the hearing impaired.

On reading about our success in *The Wall Street Journal*, the president of Encyclopaedia Britannica Films asked me to put together a workshop for his staff on how we came up with the ideas for our videos and how we developed ideas to market them. Halfway into my presentation to the Britannica executives, one of the vice presidents shouted out: "We've just come up with more ideas to solve this problem than we've had in the last three months of endless meetings." On the flight home, I realized that the creativity techniques that came so easily to me could be taught to others and, more important, needed to be taught to others. So I looked carefully at the ways creative people come up with ideas and began to compare them with my own techniques of idea making.

Slowly, over time, I began to develop a series of lectures on the nature of creativity itself and found my services in demand for training programs at Du Pont, NASA, the Federal Executive Institute, the FBI Training Academy, General Electric, Philip Morris, and a host of other companies and government agencies.

Teaching these courses to a variety of executives convinced me that my methods of idea making do work and should be available to a wider audience.

Hence, this book. Here I commit to paper my notion of what creativity is all about and my ways of actively coming up with great ideas. In the pages that follow, you will learn some theory and some practical idea-making exercises you can use in your daily professional life. You will also find a host of Great Idea Action Sheets, which I encourage you to use in meetings, on bulletin boards, on airplane flights, and even at home to help your kids with their homework.

Great ideas don't belong just to creative giants; we all live in the forest of creativity, where great ideas are as natural and accessible as the sun.

Chapter 2

READY, FIRE . . . AIM!
The Origin of Ideas

One of the most commonly asked questions in my seminars on creativity is "Where do ideas come from?" In an academic text, I'd be tempted to say that ideas come from "divergent thinking." But because I'm not writing an academic text, I prefer to say that great ideas come from:

"Ready, Fire . . . Aim!" Thinking

Traditionally, many people would say that ideas come from brainstorming. But successful brainstorming often involves much more than our typical image of the process assumes. "Ready, Fire . . . Aim!" brainstorming follows a one-two-three process—and can follow these steps on at least three different levels. The steps:

1. *Define your problem [READY].*

2. *Come up with as many ideas as you can as fast as you can without criticizing them [FIRE].*

3. *Sift, synthesize, and choose [AIM].*

Creativity consists of coming up with many ideas, not just that one great idea. These ideas typically are not focused at the time you conceive them. They are not anticipated. They are not, in a word, "aimed." They don't come with teeth-clenched concentration. They don't require "effort" in their creation. Idea making, then, requires you, the Idea Person, to get ready, fire away, wait for the smoke to clear, and then look around to see if you hit anything worthwhile. Look at all the ideas lying around and see whether any seem promising. If none are any good, get ready, fire again, blast away, and then . . . aim. Maybe this time you hit something.

This approach is a hybrid of "divergent" and "convergent" thinking. Instead of concentrating inwardly on a problem or goal, the divergent thinker looks elsewhere for solutions: up, down, under, over, far away, backward, inside out, outside in, in the clouds, in myths, in dreams. The divergent thinker looks for the vision and tries to see the problem solved. The divergent thinker plays strange mental games and may imagine a refrigerator in dire need of two boxes of baking soda, one for the veggies and one for the ice cream!

I've noticed that brainstorming often occurs on three levels, each more sophisticated than the last, and that these tend to move from convergent to divergent in approach.

> *Ideas usually don't come by "aiming" for them with teeth-clenched concentration. They don't require "effort."*

Level One of brainstorming seems to be a sharing of facts and experiences. Here, "Ready, Fire . . . Aim!" doesn't yet involve throwing out ideas that strike the people offering them as great "aha!" discoveries. But this level is what I think most people mean by brainstorming. It could be called "convergent firing"—narrowly aimed, like the shot from a .22 rifle.

On Level Two, we look around and realize that even though we've thrown out everything we knew, we need to come up with something new and different. That's when we're inspired to fire away in the unpredictable, divergent pattern I've described, like the shot from a shotgun. The first level is based on what we know and isn't really original, but on the second level we don't know where the process is going or what it might yield. To succeed, the process has got to create a universal "aha"; the answer typically will be new, original, and unexpected even to the person who comes up with it.

Level Three is a wild one where we not only don't know where the process is going, we don't know where the reframing or main idea came from. These are the kinds of flashes that happen while one is commuting or taking a shower—what I might call higher-level self-brainstorming. It doesn't happen very often in groups; it's probably what artists, writers, and musicians tend to experience.

When Hanley Norins, formerly a creative director of the Young & Rubicam advertising agency, asked other successful advertising people how they came up with ideas, "almost to a man and woman, they said, through free association." The importance of free association in the "Fire" phase of "Ready, Fire . . . Aim!" lies in the word *free*. A Young & Rubicam creative director once compared the creative process to a sponge soaking up information, which is followed by "the squeeze part: when you wring out the sponge and scribble down the most promising splashes and driblets" (Hanley Norins, *The Young & Rubicam Traveling Creative Workshop* [Englewood Cliffs, N.J.: Prentice-Hall, 1990]). However, in "Ready, Fire . . . Aim!" you write down everything, and only then choose what's promising.

Many people use only a convergent method of idea making. They look at what's wrong with their situation, their environment, their company, their boss, their organization, their spouse. By focusing on the current state of affairs, they tend to limit their view of the

CREATIVE RULE OF THUMB #3

Always look for a second right answer.

possibilities. By trying to come up with a solution, they often actively prevent solutions. By using only analytical and deductive reasoning, they force themselves down the rigid path of linear reasoning. The perils of this path were summed up by philosopher Emile Chartier:

> *Nothing is more dangerous than an idea when it's the only one you have.*

We've all known "monomaniacs," people hell-bent on one way to do something. Monomaniacs are quite likely to have that one great scheme that's so good they won't breathe a word about it unless you sign some sort of nondisclosure form. For contrast, one need only remember Dr. NakaMats and his openness to new ideas and his willingness to display his own.

A better way to achieve creativity is "Ready, Fire . . . Aim!" Rather than encourage you to draw your wagons into a circle around one or two precious ideas, this approach allows you to be open to many ideas. And it helps make the idea-creating process a way of life. It emphasizes the joy of idea making, rather than the misery that would come from trying to "get" that one idea that will somehow change everything. Creators derive their satisfactions from diving into the river of creativity and swimming—from the creative life itself.

Creating an Idea-Friendly Environment

Highly creative people are quite attuned to those times and places in which they come up with their best ideas. Dr. NakaMats, for example, travels from his "static" room to his "dynamic" room and finally to his "wet" room all in his daily pursuit of a new idea for another patentable invention.

Other great thinkers, writers, and inventors have had their own times and places for their best creating. Hemingway wrote in cafés during the early morning. Duke Ellington wrote his music on trains. Descartes worked in bed. Edison slept in his lab so he could write down ideas when they came to him, even in the dead of night. Beethoven carried a notebook around with him to write down ideas for compositions.

Others have come on their ideas by surprise and were simply ready to recognize the moment when it arrived. They had prepared the ground for innovation; they had created an idea-friendly environment. In 1890, Friedrich von Kekule, a professor of chemistry, had been attempting to solve the structure of the benzene molecule. He fell asleep in a chair and dreamed of a serpent eating its own tail. That dream evolved into the closed carbon ring structure that revolutionized organic chemistry. Painters commonly recognize the value of "accidents" in their work, and of course a multitude of inventions have been discovered "by accident," while the inventor was trying to produce something else.

Even those of us who are not in the same league with the great thinkers of Western civilization know that some times and some places are more conducive to creating than others. When you're driving down the road, suddenly something strikes and, in a fraction of a moment, you solve that problem that's been nagging at you all day. Or you're taking a shower, and, almost without knowing it, you come up with a brilliant plan. Creativity just seems to be encouraged at certain times or in certain places.

And even though we might not rank with the world's great thinkers, we can benefit by following their example and establishing idea-friendly times and places.

Idea-Friendly Times

In my creativity workshops, I've conducted informal surveys of the most idea-friendly times.

Counting down, the top ten are:

10. *While performing manual labor.*

9. *While listening to a church sermon.*

8. *On waking up in the middle of the night.*

7. *While exercising.*

6. *During leisure reading.*

5. *During a boring meeting.*

4. *While falling asleep or waking up.*

3. *While commuting to work.*

2. *While showering or shaving.*

1. *While sitting on the toilet!*

If you should doubt that the throne heads the list of the most creative times, consider the new and highly profitable advertising business known as Headlines USA. Based in Houston, Texas, this rapidly growing specialty advertising firm strategically places "print medium" advertising, in both His and Hers versions, before an audience held captive . . . in public restrooms! The founder of the company reports that he was struck with the inspiration "while reading a newspaper that was framed and posted above the facilities in a Houston restaurant."

And at NASA's base in Ames, California, someone has thoughtfully provided holders for 3" x 5" cards bolted to the walls of toilet stalls. Close by are pens hanging on chains.

You, of course, should search your own habits and identify those times when you tend to come up with the best ideas. Chances are that your idea-friendliest time won't be while sitting at your desk straining to come up with something clever. Then, when you need some great ideas, maximize your chances by seeking out those idea-friendly times. As Albert Einstein once said:

> **CREATIVE RULE OF THUMB #4**
>
> **If at first you don't succeed . . . take a break!**

Make friends with your shower. If inspired to sing, maybe the song has an idea in it for you.

Creating an idea-friendly time for yourself can be as simple as taking a break: get up from your desk, get a cup of coffee, walk to another department, or stay at your desk and accomplish a simple task on your to-do list, glance at a magazine, or look out the window. "I'll type things on the typewriter," an ad agency creative director says, "random thoughts. The act of typing . . . helps me get loose, the way a runner warms up before a race" (Norins, *The Young & Rubicam Traveling Creative Workshop*). Nancy Badore, Director of Ford Motor Company's Executive Development Center, uses her commute time to recharge her creative batteries. As recounted in *The Female Advantage: Women's Ways of Leadership* by Sally Helgesen (New York: Doubleday Currency, 1990), Badore says that she is "very conscious of letting my brain wander and float while I'm driving. I don't turn the radio on, I don't concentrate on tasks I have to do. The day's so fast-paced, it's hard to find time to totally tune out; I do that in the car, and find I have some of my most creative moments while driving on the highway."

The creator of the award-winning flying machine, the *Gossamer Condor*, and most recently the General Motors solar-powered *Sunraycer*, credits daydreaming for his inspiration. Paul MacCready cites a month-long, seven-thousand-mile driving vacation and endless hours of watching red-tailed hawks as primary factors leading to his design of the *Gossamer Condor*, which now hangs in the Smithsonian next to the Wright brothers' first airplane.

Record Your Ideas

As you begin to focus on your idea-friendly times and on ways to heighten your creativity, you've got to be ready to write your ideas down. Otherwise, if you're like many creative people, you'll forget your ideas before you have a chance to act. Have you ever had a great idea just as you woke up in the morning, but when you got to the office, it was gone? Many ideas are directly tied to their environment of origin. Change the environment, and the idea goes away. To prevent this loss of your great ideas, get in the habit of writing them down.

The following are some of the methods I've used to record my ideas:

1. *Put a pad of paper by your bed or in your kitchen.*

2. *Keep a grease pencil in your shower. It comes off with any liquid cleaner.*

3. Drive with a cassette recorder in your glove compartment.

4. Carry 3" x 5" cards in your pocket or carry a small notebook.

5. Write it down in your TV Guide.

6. Use a mnemonic device, by making a pictorial association with the essence of your idea.

7. Phone your answering service or machine and leave a message.

8. Write it on your wrist.

9. Don't forget a pen or pencil. If you forget, be creative and use dust on your dashboard, steam on your bathroom mirror, or sand on the beach.

Create an Idea Bank

The Idea Note shown in this chapter is the size of a dollar bill, for saved ideas are like money in the bank. They will gain interest—your interest— as you look through them to spark even more new ideas. Print up a pad of these Idea Notes and give them to your colleagues or employees. Carry some around in your wallet for those flashes of insight and then file them away in a card box labeled "Idea Bank."

Ideas save time, make money, and are fun.

Idea Note

Idea-Friendly Places

Of course, when it's time to create, you can't always take a shower, run to the john, or commute to work. At least not without creating quite a stir in the office. So you must pay attention to your surroundings, to the place where you hang your hat most of the day or night, and see whether it promotes or retards the creative process. Of immediate concern, and the place over which you exert considerable control, is, most likely, your office.

Take a look around. Is your office a friend or foe to the creative process?

Define your office, even if only in terms of negatives. For example, your office is not a garbage can, so it should be free from clutter, piled-up papers, and old Twinkies wrappers. Are your visitor chairs filled with old newspapers so that people are discouraged from coming in, having a seat, and chewing the fat (an often fertile source of great ideas)?

Is your office a trophy case adorned with awards, degrees, and other testimonials to your past performance? Does it contain any monuments to your future? Do your degrees on the wall really impress your visitors? Perhaps they are necessary displays of knowledge and competence to reassure a paying client, but if no paying clients visit your office, perhaps your degrees intimidate and thwart those who do come by for a visit. Most of all, perhaps they dull your own sense of your present and future.

> *Is your office a trophy case adorned with testimonials to your past performance? Does it contain any monuments to your future?*

Although your office probably shouldn't be your fortress, you might consider actively keeping people and other intrusions out during some parts of the day. Former Governor Gerald Baliles of Virginia, who was widely considered to be unusually innovative and effective in his job, allowed no appointments before ten o'clock each morning or after four o'clock each afternoon. He used the time to reflect and to consider his options in a relaxed environment.

To help you make your office a place that invites the creative process, here are some suggestions, all borrowed from participants in my creativity workshops.

1. *Put your baby picture on your desk facing out. Not your baby's picture, your baby picture. That's right. A picture of*

you when you were young and innocent and oh so creative! This friendly touch will open up your staff and clients to help you brainstorm new ideas. They'll realize that you weren't forty-five years old on the day you were born!

2. *Put a marker board or flip chart in your office so you can easily initiate "Ready, Fire . . . Aim!" sessions when a colleague or employee brings in a problem.*

3. *Spend $5 for something on your desk to represent your vision. I've used this device in my creativity workshops with managers. Here are some items purchased by workshop participants: a toy fire hydrant ("I put out fires!"), a jar full of cat's-eye marbles ("I'm keeping an eye on the future!"), a picture of Mickey Mouse ("To remind me of the incredible customer service at Walt Disney World!").*

4. *Find and hang a picture of your vision on your wall. NASA has lots of pictures of space stations and the moon. Bob Stripling, city manager of Roanoke, Virginia, who wanted a new downtown parking garage, hung pictures of award-winning parking garages in his office as a reminder of his vision and as a prompter of ideas necessary to reach that vision.*

5. *Put some toys on your desk—Legos, a box of Crayola crayons, and other childlike toys to remind you of the innocence and simplicity of creativity. You'll be amazed at how many of your visitors pick them up and play with them.*

6. *No office is complete without a Gary Larson* Far Side *book on the same table as your issues of* Harvard Business Review.

Creating an Idea-Friendly Office Environment

I'm not an expert in "space management," but physical surroundings certainly affect the mood and, therefore, the creativity of people in those surroundings. Drab, dreary offices with little light, bad ventilation, no plants, and oppressive walls are not likely to bring forth a flow of free thought and discussion. If you have power over conditions beyond the four walls of your office, you should give considerable thought to whether or not your entire organization operates in an idea-friendly environment. If it doesn't, the time to change is now.

As a starting point, you might consider exchanging your ordinary fluorescent lights for full-spectrum fluorescents or incandescent table lamps, bringing in some real or high-quality silk plants, and providing some background music, preferably the largo movements from classical and baroque composers. Why largo? Because the cadence is slower than the average heartbeat. This music has been found to improve concentration and accelerate learning.

Creating an Idea-Friendly Office: Speed and "Junk Work"

If you're burdened by pointless reports, endless meetings, redundant approvals, you're not alone. In a recent poll, 74 percent of executives find themselves mired in outdated, counterproductive methods of doing business, bogged down in the 11.25 million meetings they attend every day in the United States—more than 70 million worldwide—and smothered by yet another report that probably belongs in the trash can.

Today's successful public and private organizations are making decisions faster, developing new products and services earlier, and delivering those products and services sooner than their competitors. One key to success in today's world is speed, for it's been proven again and again that time is money—more money earned or less money spent.

According to Jack Welch, CEO of General Electric, "For a large organization to be competitive, it must have Speed, Simplicity, and Self-Confidence." Simply put, today's global organization has to be able to deliver services anytime, anywhere, to anyone, no matter what. That's customer satisfaction for the 1990s.

Speed, however, is not necessarily "stepping on the gas," doing everything the same way, only faster. In fact, speed can involve slowing down, taking an in-depth look at the way your organization is doing things, and asking, "How can we do this in half the time?"

Speed comes from simplification of the function of both the organization as a whole and of each employee. Jack Welch asks executives to compile a list of the twenty things they're doing that make them work seventy hours each week. "I bet five of them are 'junk work' and can be eliminated," he says.

And how does an employee pinpoint junk work? In his book *Information Anxiety* (New York: Doubleday, 1989), Richard Saul Wurman may have the perfect illustration. Every executive reads and writes reports. What each has to do is recognize the difference between information and data. Wurman says that today's work world is experiencing a "data explosion, not an information explosion. The total number of bytes or bits of stuff being produced or sitting around has increased. The value of it, in terms of what is really there that's of any function or utility, has not increased." In other words, every executive has to determine if the facts, figures, and numbers in the parade of reports mean anything to the organization's future. Data that have no significance beyond the page they're printed on amount to junk work.

> **CREATIVE RULE OF THUMB #5**
>
> **Write down your ideas before you forget them!**

For speed to increase, junk work must be eliminated. Instead of controlling, managers need to learn to work with and trust the organization and must develop the self-confidence to peel away managerial layers. As Welch says, "For a large organization to be effective, its people must have self-confidence and intellectual self-assurance. Insecure managers create complexity" (Noel Tichy and Ram Charan, "Speed, Simplicity, Self-Confidence: An Interview with Jack Welch," *Harvard Business Review*, September–October 1989).

Hewlett-Packard is one company that wanted to trim down and speed up and did. John Young, chief executive officer, announced that he would cut by a full 50 percent his company's breakeven time (the time between a product's conceptualization and its ultimate profitability). The cost of such speedy work is higher, initially. The effect of such innovation on employees, however, is exhilarating. "My workers like the challenge," Young says. "They like to win at business. That's why they're here" (Beverly Geber, "Speed: Where the People Fit In," *Training*, August 1989). And that's why Hewlett-Packard continues to be innovative and continues to be profitable.

Another sign of the times is the recent effort by Toyota to crack open its hierarchical tradition and allow an easier, faster flow of ideas. The corporation has cycled half of its white-collar managers back into work on the front line, shifted the basis of promotions and raises from seniority toward merit, and drastically cut down on the number of approvals needed for a new idea.

So look around you. Challenge everything you do, every report you write (or read), your ordinary way of getting through the day. What in your routine aids the creative process? More important, what actually hinders the free flow of great ideas? What do you do during the day that slows you down? What gets in your way? Lost phone numbers? Forgotten messages? Misfiled reports? Junk work?

The removal of hindrances and junk work certainly plays a vital role in promoting the creative process. These steps signal that an organization's priority is innovation, not defensiveness. On the smallest scale, creating an idea-friendly office can be a good first step in stripping away obstacles to performance and barriers to great ideas.

A Climate for Creativity

Creativity, then, comes from a process, a way of thinking and of looking at the world, a way of approaching problems. Creativity rises from the unexpected: from a clash of opposites, from metaphors, from dreams of the future. A creative office environment recognizes these ways of creative thinking and tries to encourage them through design and decor. If your "busy executives" say they can't afford to leave their desks, you might remember the notion of idea-friendly times or you might challenge that assumption and say that "busy execs can't afford not to leave their desks." You might indeed try to design an environment that nudges people away from their desks and into more idea-friendly times and places.

Steelcase, Inc., the large office furniture company, saw that as a maker of "office environments," it had to come up with a creative environment of its own for its new corporate development center in Grand Rapids, Michigan. They engaged top organizational psychologists and charged them with designing a physical layout that would encourage "the formal and informal interaction of both people and ideas," and encourage "both planned and spontaneous communication and teamwork."

The innovative interior design of Steelcase's new $111 million, pyramid-shaped Corporate Development Center features break areas, "neighborhoods," and an executive cluster. The break areas, informal areas to foster impromptu meetings, are strategically positioned between neighborhoods throughout the building. All break areas are equipped with marker boards, coffee, and soft drinks. In the words of Dr. Thomas Allen, the MIT organizational psychologist commissioned to design the facility, the break areas are furnished "to promote random interaction of people and ideas as well as immediate reaction and feedback to spontaneous thoughts and action."

"We're moving from the relay team to the rugby team approach to product development," was the way Steelcase president and CEO Frank H. Merlotti described the overall importance of the company's pyramid. "We're getting everybody involved up front and letting them lock in like a rugby team does, all moving toward the goal."

The building's design forces interaction between top management and the creative research-and-development process. The company even coined the term *functional inconvenience* to describe the effect of requiring people from different departments and disciplines to intermingle.

Steelcase accomplished through architecture what Philip L. Smith, chairman of General Foods, seeks in his organization:

> *Talking between research, manufacturing, and sales must be forced. It does not come naturally. Progress is more important than secrecy. You put more at risk by not talking.*

Creating idea-friendly environments can also be accomplished organizationally. In his book *From Vision to Reality: Strategies of Successful Innovators in Government* (Charlottesville, Va.: LEL Enterprises, 1990), Dr. Russell Linden recounts the successes of Jim Colvard, a top manager in the U.S. Navy who created a revolutionary organizational structure that fostered a high degree of creativity. Colvard rotated his department heads every three to four years, moving each senior manager to head a brand new department, and required them to sit on a "board of directors" to make organizationwide decisions. By changing the actual perspective of these senior managers, Colvard helped them achieve a more "corporate" perspective, reducing turf building and other mind-sets that often retard creativity and change.

An essential part of Jack Welch's campaign at GE has been the creation of a much freer corporate environment—where "three hundred thousand people with different career objectives, different family aspirations, different financial goals . . . share directly in this company's vision, the decision-making process, and the rewards" and where "accomplishment is rewarded in both the pocketbook and the soul."

Easy Ways to Start

Of course, you might lack $111 million to build a new corporate development center. But lack of funds shouldn't deter you. Change your offices around, create spaces where people congregate, allow them to interact. Rename your meeting or break areas to fit your vision. Apple Computer named its meeting rooms "Dorothy" and "Toto" to let everybody know that a wizard dwells within each person. Or change your organization around. Encourage your managers to see different perspectives, to interact with different people.

Creating an idea-friendly environment can be as simple as letting people know that you encourage the creation of great ideas. So pass around pads of Idea Notes and encourage people to deposit them in their Idea Banks.

Remember: Writing down your new ideas is money in the bank!

Chapter 3

KILLER PHRASES
The Enemies of Ideas

The innovator has for enemies all who have done well under the old, and lukewarm defenders in those who may do well under the new.

—*Machiavelli, 1513*

You know that no idea is any good until someone does something with it or to it. Someone has to accept it, adopt it, run with it, put it into action. That someone, of course, is often someone other than you. Implementing great ideas requires a team effort.

So you must tell somebody about your idea. And if you've ever tried to bring up new ideas to other people, you know that although your idea could be met with thunderous applause, it may just as easily elicit derisive laughter, or perhaps just a shrug.

What determines the success or failure of your idea? Two things. The quality of the idea and the quality of its promotion. If the idea turns out to be unworkable, then you want failure. You want the idea to fail—fast. If it doesn't fail fast, count on it eating up precious time and resources. But assuming your idea is a good one, what is it out there that just might make it fail anyway and shoot it down before it has the slightest chance to spread its wings? In fact, what do you *know* will happen to your great idea as soon as you suggest it to your boss, colleague, spouse, or other important person in your life? Somebody, somewhere, at some time, will come up, gun loaded, aim, and say . . .

"It's not in the budget."

"We don't do it that way."

"We've tried that before."

Bang! Bang! Bang!

Somebody shoots down your great idea with *Killer Phrases*. And Killer Phrases just might do in your great idea, before it even gets on track.

Idea Generators must learn all about Killer Phrases, for they are as inevitable in the innovation process as ideas themselves. Successful Idea Generators must learn what these phrases are, where they come from, when they are likely to rear their ugly heads, and how they might best be overcome. Psychologists have said that the human reaction to a new idea unfolds something like this, which we could call the Five Stages of Idea Acceptance:

1. It's irrelevant to this situation.

2. It's relevant, but it's unproven.

3. It's proven, but it's dangerous.

4. It's safe, but it's not sellable.

5. It'll sell, what a great idea!

From conception to fruition, successful ideas tend to follow a path of ultimate but grudging acceptance. All along the way, Killer Phrases dive in from all angles, seeking to obstruct, demean, diminish, counteract.

Killer Phrases have been around since the dawn of time. They are uttered by seers, pundits, pessimists, naysayers, doomsayers, leaders, bosses, husbands, wives, siblings, coaches, writers, teachers . . . indeed, by everyone, including you. They've become part of our history, part of our culture, and as you will soon see, part of our language. Consider ex-President Grover Cleveland's astute observation in 1905:

"Sensible and responsible women do not want the right to vote."

Harry Warner, president of Warner Brothers, said in 1927:

"Who the hell wants to hear actors talk!"

Decca Records pronounced, when it turned down the Beatles in 1962:

"Groups with guitars are on their way out."

Consider, as I sit here in my home and compose this book on my computer, the words uttered in 1977 by a computer manufacturer:

"There is no reason for any individual to have a computer in his home."

A very recent Killer Phrase was hurled at those considering business relationships with the Soviet Union:

"Their currency isn't convertible!"

PepsiCo and Ben & Jerry's ice cream didn't let that stop them. They overcame the convertibility problem by devising unique systems of barter:

> *One bottle of Pepsi = three-quarters of an ounce of Stolichnaya vodka*

> *One bottle of Pepsi = fifteen-billionths of a ship*

> *One ice cream cone = one-hundredth of a Matroiska nesting doll (plus some walnuts and honey thrown in for good measure).*

> *At home, parents utter 18 negative statements for every positive one—usually to an inquisitive child who wants to know how something works.*

Killer Phrases are part of our culture, part of our upbringing. One study showed that negative *no-can-do* statements are all around us, outweighing positive *can-do* statements by substantial margins. At home, parents say, on average, 18 negative statements for every one positive statement they utter, usually to a naturally inquisitive child trying to find out how something works. The average is 432 negative statements per day! "Don't touch. Don't play with that." The same study showed that teachers display a 12-to-1 ratio of negative statements to positive ones, perhaps to students eager to answer or ask a question. "Be still. Don't talk. Don't do that." In the national media, the ratio of negative stories—murder, mayhem, corruption, scandal—to positive stories is, surprisingly, lower, but still weighs in at 6 to 1.

Killer Phrases are part of our language. All around us, practically from our first breath, we're bombarded by them. Often, they really do get in our way.

They certainly get in our way in business or government organizations. When I hear managers flinging a lot of Killer Phrases, I'm often reminded of seagulls. I'm reminded of Seagull Management—the act of swooping in on unsuspecting office staff, dumping unpleasant information on them, and then flying away. There's also the Seagull Consultant, who swoops in, eats your food, dumps on you, and then flies away.

But negative assumptions are such an ingrained part of organizational life that they can probably be considered a kind of corporate neurotic syndrome and one that is ultimately self-defeating. Peter Senge, in his book *The Fifth Discipline: The Art & Practice of the Learning Organization* (New York: Doubleday Currency, 1990), says that "learning disabilities . . . are fatal in organizations. Because of them, few corporations live even half as long as a person—most die before they reach the age of forty." Surely the Killer Phrase is symptomatic of an inability or refusal to learn.

William E. Perry, executive director of the Quality Assurance Institute, calls this syndrome "the 'No' Response"—and finds that the "No" Response squelches creativity and effectiveness throughout the federal government. He observes that the three most typical responses of a federal manager, all beginning with "No, we can't do it," are

1. *"The law prohibits it."*

2. *"We've always done it another way."*

3. *"We don't have any money."*

All of them "generally mean that the manager does not want to take the time or does not have the interest in exploring the issue or proposal being raised" (William E. Perry, "Managers Can Unlearn the 'No' Response," *Government Computer News*, December 10, 1990).

Noting that Toyota now implements an average of forty suggestions per employee per year, Perry wonders what would happen if the federal government did the same. "What could that do to the effectiveness and efficiency of government operations?" Opening management's attitude, he says, "means installing a total quality management system." I believe that this is a critical point, because the Killer Phrase, in squashing creativity, kills quality, efficiency, and all the improvements that could lead to savings, profits, higher morale and a better quality of life.

"The Top 40" is a list of Killer Phrases I've collected in my creativity workshops:

Killer Phrases: The Top 40

1. "Yes, but . . ."
2. "We tried that before."
3. "That's irrelevant."
4. "We haven't got the manpower."
5. "Obviously, you misread my request."
6. "Don't rock the boat!"
7. "The boss (or competition) will eat you alive."
8. "Don't waste time thinking."
9. "Great idea, but not for us."
10. "It'll never fly."
11. "Don't be ridiculous."
12. "People don't want change."
13. "It's not in the budget."
14. "Put it in writing."
15. "It will be more trouble than it's worth."
16. "It isn't your responsibility."
17. "That's not in your job description."
18. "You can't teach an old dog new tricks."
19. "Let's stick with what works."
20. "We've done all right so far."
21. "The boss will never go for it."
22. "It's too far ahead of the times."
23. . . . laughter . . .
24. . . . suppressed laughter . . .
25. . . . condescending grin . . .
26. . . . dirty looks . . .
27. "Don't fight city hall!"
28. "I'm the one who gets paid to think."
29. "What will people say?"
30. "Get a committee to look into that."
31. "If it ain't broke, don't fix it."
32. "You have got to be kidding."
33. "No!"
34. "We've always done it this way."
35. "It's all right in theory . . . but . . ."
36. "Be practical!"
37. "Do you realize the paperwork it will create?"
38. "Because I said so."
39. "I'll get back to you."
40. . . . silence . . .

Send Me Your Killer Phrases

In the appendix you'll find how you can receive a free Killer Phrase poster for each *unique* Killer Phrase you send in that we use in our next book. If we already have that one on file, sorry, we can't send the poster.

You will, however, receive a thank-you letter. When we get enough responses, naturally, we'll publish the sequel: *What a Great Idea Part II!*

Why Killer Phrases?

> *Truth emerges from the clash of adverse ideas.*
> — John Stuart Mill

Although Killer Phrases do perform some useful functions—preventing precipitous, mindless change, protecting us from potential danger—they also squelch good ideas, retard progress, inhibit innovation. They come from a human being's natural reluctance to change. They come from an organization's preference for doing things in established patterns, using known procedures and habitual policies. They come from society's tendency to cling to the known and to fear the unknown, the untried, the new. The natural reluctance will always manifest itself as a hurdle to new ideas—kind of a natural "innovation review board" before which all new ideas must pass.

> **CREATIVE RULE OF THUMB #6**
>
> **If everyone says you're wrong, you're one step ahead. If everyone laughs at you, you're two steps ahead.**

Each of us—even the high-flying optimists, the Cheerleaders of this world—has some degree of reluctance to change. If we did not, if we threw caution to the wind, we'd no doubt get into real trouble. Others of us, the most dogged pessimists, the Booleaders—as I call them—have an overabundance of love for things as they are and an unhealthy fear of new and exciting ideas. The Booleader will always look for what's wrong with an idea, no matter how attractive it might look to everyone else. Even after a great idea is being implemented, even after everyone else has endorsed it, the Booleader is over there sulking, hoping for failure, hoping for that chance to say, "I told you so." Every organization has a little bevy of Booleaders, and the Idea Generator must beware, for the Booleaders are the quickest ones to fling Killer Phrases.

The Cheerleaders, on the other hand, might fall in love with every new idea and be blinded to their shortcomings. They might close their minds to responsible criticism from others and plunge headlong toward disaster.

What we need, of course, is cooperation between these two opposing forces. The natural Booleaders should withhold premature criticism until the idea has a chance to grow and prove itself. The Cheerleaders should know when to stop promoting and begin to listen to realistic criticism from others.

Internalized Killer Phrases

Killer Phrases can occur throughout the idea-generation process. Even while an idea is cooking, the Idea Generator is often filled with self-doubt; often *we* are the source of the most destructive negative assumptions. How many times, during the course of a plan, have you said, "I'll look stupid" or "Somebody has already done it" or "I don't have time." These are "Internalized Killer Phrases." How often have you had a great idea but failed to follow through? How often have you put off writing that memo needed to change a system or try a new strategy? When was the last time you started working on a project but talked yourself out of going any farther with it?

The Idea Generator must be careful of Internalized Killer Phrases, which can stamp out the creative process before it even begins. They come in a variety of shapes and sizes:

Self-Doubt Killer Phrases

I'm not old enough. I'm not experienced enough. I'm not good enough, tall enough, fast enough, forceful enough, young enough, creative enough.

I say to myself, "Chic, why not treat yourself as your own best friend rather than as your own worst enemy. Be creative. After all, would your best friend say that you couldn't meet the challenge or that you're not creative enough?" Remember the words of Eleanor Roosevelt, "No one can make you feel inferior without your consent."

Excuse Killer Phrases

I haven't got enough disk space to finish that chapter now, so I'll wait until tomorrow. I'd better prepare some more before I make that presentation to the board. I need copies, but the copier's down, so I'll wait until it's fixed.

I say to myself, "It's better to be proactive than reactive. Get it done, even if it requires revision."

Procrastination Killer Phrases

I'll finish this first and then, tomorrow, I can start that report I wanted to do today. Tomorrow just makes more sense. It's better to wait and see what happens tomorrow.

I say to myself, "Just do it or forget about it!"

Fear Killer Phrases

I don't want to offend anybody. They won't like my idea. Nobody ever pays any attention to what I have to say.

These might be perfectly legitimate. After all, the natural reluctance to change is like a societal survival instinct. But if the fear is an irrational reluctance to take a risk, these Killer Phrases will kill you as well.

I say to myself, "I learn by trial and error, not by trial and accuracy." Thomas Carlisle said, "Our greatest glory is not in never failing, but in rising every time we fall."

How to Overcome Internalized Killer Phrases

You're trying to solve a problem or reach a goal, but the Killer Phrases inside your own head are getting in the way. Self-doubt, excuses, procrastination, and fear all haunt you daily, impeding your progress, hurting your chances for success. What can you do? Lots of things.

Positive affirmations do help overcome self-doubt. Post an affirmation like "I believe in myself" on your bathroom mirror or refrigerator door. You'll find that successful people do this all the time. They pause to remember those silent, determined statements that keep them going. Is it corny? Sure. Does it work? Ask any successful athlete or salesperson.

Try games of opposites. If self-doubt nags at you and threatens to snuff out creativity, then write down all the negative phrases you use over and over again. Put your list in the left-hand column on a sheet of paper. Like this:

Too young.

Not enough education.

No time.

Then write down the opposites of these negative statements in a right-hand column:

Too young.	*Too old.*
Not enough education.	*Too much education.*
No time.	*Too much time.*

Reality, of course, probably lies somewhere between these two extremes, but you've been focusing on only one side. Perhaps you're really "*almost* too young." Well, then, what other traits do you have that can overcome this shortcoming, a shortcoming that might only be self-perceived?

Diffusing External Killer Phrases

When you create great ideas, you must then be prepared to encounter and overcome External Killer Phrases. Overcoming these, many of which undoubtedly appear on the Top 40 chart, requires a systematic approach.

The challenge for the Idea Generator is to diffuse the Killer Phrase—to divert it, to deflect it, to neutralize it before it gets you. Although I might be tempted to say we "defuse" Killer Phrases—attack them, in effect, removing their power—I prefer to talk about "diffusing" them, because it's a less confrontational term. As you'll see, it's possible to let negativity collapse under its own weight, while you persist in making certain your idea gets the hearing it deserves.

> *The Idea Generator needs to divert and neutralize Killer Phrases before they do lasting damage.*

Step One

Identify the typical Killer Phrases around you, for chances are they've been institutionalized. By knowing in advance what the negative responses are likely to be, you can more readily devise a plan of counterattack or accommodation. For example, I'm prepared for new clients to say, "But we tried that before and it failed miserably," when I recommend combining salaried and hourly employees in the same training session. I'm also prepared to hear "But it's not in the budget" when I suggest follow-up training and train-the-trainer sessions.

Step Two

When you encounter a Killer Phrase, you must determine its source. Find out right away if it's coming from a Booleader. If so, you must realize that such a person *always* reacts this way to *any* new idea that anybody *else* offers. Strategy: Proceed to Step Three to get more information and to Steps Four and Five to plan a sales strategy for your idea.

Step Three

Examine the Killer Phrase and see whether or not the person is simply asking a question. For example, "It's not in the budget" might be the disguised question "How much will it cost?" "We've tried that before" might be the disguised question "What's new and different about your approach?" If the Killer Phrase is really a question, the strategy is simple: Answer it.

Step Four

Figure out whether the person flinging the Killer Phrase at you has *more* decision-making power than you do. Quite obviously, if this person is your boss or occupies a higher position in the organization, then his or her beliefs and power to make decisions can be terminal to your bright idea. Indeed, those higher up in the organization are paid to be skeptical. They want good ideas, that's for sure. But they also want to unearth bad ideas to see that they fail and fail fast. Assuming your idea is a good one, your strategy becomes: Sell upward.

To sell upward, first and foremost, you've got to broaden your political base. One way is to identify the person who's likely to provide the strongest opposition, in an attempt to diffuse anticipated Killer Phrases before they arise. Approach an associate of this potential foe, show the associate the merit of the idea, try to win the associate over to your point of view. If you do, then approach the likely foe with your idea *before* you float the idea before the organization as a whole.

Selling upward requires you to marshal your political forces, to capture their imagination, to seek the input and assistance of others, and to anticipate their concerns and potential objections.

Another strategy in dealing with Killer Phrases hurled from above might be one of defiance. In the late 1960s, an engineer at Hewlett-Packard (H-P) was developing a computer graphics display system. Top management felt the system had limited sales potential, so on an annual lab inspection tour, they told the young engineer, "We don't want to see any signs of this project on our next lab visit." The engineer decided to interpret this Killer Phrase to mean: "Hurry up, produce it, and get it out of the development stage."

Chuck House did just that, and eventually his graphics display system became a big moneymaker for H-P. House was awarded the first H-P Medal of Defiance.

> *Management told a young engineer they didn't want to see any sign of his project on their next visit; he took that to mean "Hurry up and produce it!"*

Companies that truly encourage their people to buck the system are still in the minority. Leadership expert Warren Bennis maintains that at least seven out of ten employees in American companies keep quiet when their opinions are at odds with those of their superiors.

Systems for rewarding those who dare to stand up and say "I've got a better way" are still news today. However, as more walls come down and competition keeps increasing, finding a better way will be in everyone's job description.

Step Five

Figure out whether the person flinging the Killer Phrase at you has *less* decision-making power than you do. You must be ready to diffuse Killer Phrases coming from your employees, your subordinates, or others lower on the organizational chart. An idea requiring team effort and opposed by members of that team is doomed to failure. The strategy: Sell downward. People in lower positions fear change because:

1. *They might not have the skills for a faster-paced operation.*

2. *Their job might be eliminated.*

3. *They might be near to retirement.*

4. *They think this change is only a temporary whim—just another program.*

To buy in, they must see direction from above, support for possible failure, a tie-in with the mission of the company, and rewards for their successful completion of this idea. Both selling upward and selling downward require a positive presentation of your idea, encouragement of the participation of others, and a demonstration that everybody wins.

Five Ways to Overcome Killer Phrases

Managers attending my creativity workshops report that Killer Phrases arise in every organization, often in meetings. When someone brings up a suggestion or proposes a new approach, someone else shoots it down. The process, if continued and institutionalized within the organization, will thwart creative efforts and reduce the likelihood of beneficial change.

"Don't ROCK the BOAT!"

To overcome this tendency, my workshop participants have devised unique approaches to make the opposite happen, to turn the skepticism of the group not toward the Idea Generator but toward the Killer Phrase flinger. These approaches tend to turn attitudes away from "why we can't" to "why we can."

1. Institutionalize the Term "Killer Phrase"

You must first make everyone around you accustomed to the term "Killer Phrase," which should be as recognizable as the phrases themselves. Only when people recognize such responses will they be able to overcome them and prevent the destructive effects such phrases can have on an organization's creative energy.

I recommend sending out a memo declaring war on Killer Phrases along with an Action Sheet requesting help in collecting your organization's top Killer Phrases. Below is a draft of a memo for you to put into your own words and send out to those people whose aid you seek. Attach a copy of the "Common Killer Phrases" Action Sheet on page 38 to your memo.

To: _____

From: _____

Re: Killer Phrases

Every organization develops ingrained responses to new ideas and new ways of doing things. Typically, these responses are negative and try to shoot down ideas before they have a chance to prove themselves as good ideas or even as great ideas.

I've recently been reading a book called *What a Great Idea!* It reports that all organizations have these institutionalized, negative ways of reacting to new ideas.

The author calls them "Killer Phrases." The name is apt, I believe.

I think we have similar phrases in our office, and I'd like your help in identifying the most popular Killer Phrases we use. By knowing what these are and why people reflexively fling them around, we can begin to anticipate them and perhaps reduce the harmful effects they often have.

I've started a list of Killer Phrases on the next page. Please add to the list those you hear or those you use. I'll collate the results and send out a list of the most frequently listed Killer Phrases.

Many thanks for your help.

2. The Killer Phrase Response Outline

At your next meeting, after gathering the most common Killer Phrases in your office or organization, you might want to explore ways you can overcome them. At the meeting, you should pass out the Response Outline Action Sheet (pages 39–40), a systematic approach to analyzing Killer Phrases, identifying their sources, ascertaining their legitimacy, and overcoming those that threaten creativity. Ask everyone to submit their most effective Response Outline and provide a "Comeback of the Month" award.

3. The Paper Wad

At your next meeting, hand out a supply of scrap paper. Instruct each person to wad up pieces of paper to produce an arsenal of paper wads. Then tell everyone to throw a paper wad at anyone else who utters any Killer Phrase during the meeting. Some people will start to catch themselves in the middle of saying a Killer Phrase—instruct them to throw the paper wad at themselves. You'll run a meeting you'll never forget!

Two variations: Use Nerf balls instead of paper wads. Use different-colored papers.

An Opposite Version: Use a colorful Nerf ball and whenever you want a person or a team to come up with a new idea, throw the ball at them. By tossing the ball back and forth, you'll produce an effective idea-generation session.

4. The Criminal Penalty

At your next meeting, announce a fine of 25 cents for each Killer Phrase uttered by any member of the group. Enforce the fines, save the money, and buy your team a gift with the proceeds—a motivational tape, refreshments for the next meeting, or a popcorn popper for the meeting room. For an added touch of realism, use the Killer Phrase Arrest Warrant shown below and give it to your "offenders."

KILLER PHRASE ARREST WARRANT

ISSUED TO: _____

ARRESTING OFFICER: _____

DATE OF OFFENSE: _____

OFFENDING KILLER PHRASE: _____

WITNESSETH: Whereas the above-named criminal defendant did, with malice afore-thought, utter the above-quoted Killer Phrase on the above-referenced date.

NOW THEREFORE: Said criminal defendant is hereby found guilty without benefit of trial, counsel, appeal, or bail, and is hereby fined TWENTY-FIVE CENTS, said amount hereby payable immediately to the above-named arresting officer. Bribes gladly accepted.

---

5. The Billboard

Make sure your meeting room has a flip chart or marker board. Ask the group members to list on it the twenty-five most frequently uttered Killer Phrases. Making the Killer Phrases known in advance typically will reduce their use during the meeting. Some managers in my creativity workshops have produced handsome, permanent signs in meeting rooms complete with cartoons.

Following are some cartoon-balloon Killer Phrases from my own

Killer Phrase poster that may inspire you in your sign making. (To obtain a poster, see "Wanted" in the appendix.)

Another suggestion: Hang a marker board or a legal pad next to the Killer Phrase Billboard for people to jot down other Killer Phrases or catchy comebacks to Killer Phrases.

Your Call

All techniques of diffusing Killer Phrases require a healthy self-image on your part. You are the one who must overcome internalized Killer Phrases. You, the Idea Generator, must be prepared to meet external Killer Phrases head on. You must be ready to disarm the Booleader, to answer legitimate questions, to sell your ideas up or down within the organization. So be proud of that great idea of yours. If it really is a good one and if you truly believe, then you can make sure your idea gets the chance it deserves.

Common Killer Phrases

Please add the Killer Phrases you hear around the office to the list below:

1. **It's not in the budget.** _____

2. **We've tried that before.** _____

3. **If it ain't broke, don't fix it.** _____

4. _____

5. _____

6. _____

7. _____

8. _____

9. _____

10. _____

11. _____

12. _____

13. _____

14. _____

15. _____

16. _____

17. _____

18. _____

19. _____

20. _____

What a Great Idea! Copyright © 1992 by Charles "Chic" Thompson.

Killer Phrase Response Outline

Fill in the information requested in the outline below. Write down ideas for effective responses to anticipated Killer Phrases.

Step 1 Identify and jot down three anticipated Killer Phrases.

1. _____

2. _____

3. _____

Step 2 Who will utter these phrases?

1. _____

2. _____

3. _____

Step 3 Is the Killer Phrase really a disguised question? If so, jot down the real question.

1. _____

2. _____

3. _____

Step 4 Write down short answers to these disguised questions.

1. _____

2. _____

3. _____

Step 5 Write down the name of an associate of each of the three Killer Phrase users identified in Step 2.

Killer Phrase Sayer   Associate

_____   _____

_____   _____

_____   _____

Step 6 Jot down a comeback phrase that will appeal to each of the associates in Step 5 and that will help overcome the Killer Phrases identified in Step 1.

Associate   Comeback Phrase

_____   _____

_____   _____

_____   _____

Step 7 Now jot down a suggested response or strategy to overcome the anticipated Killer Phrases identified in Step 1.

1. _____

_____

2. _____

_____

3. _____

_____

Step 8 After completing the above mental exercise, take ten deep breaths, proceed with your idea, and be ready for Killer Phrases.

CONCLUSION

The essence of creative *freedom* is the ability to gather a quantity of ideas; all the rest of the creative process flows from this all-important source of fertility. To allow a multitude, a kaleidoscope of ideas requires the ability to identify and overcome those deadly assumptions we've called Killer Phrases. We've discussed a number of ways you can "fire" off ideas and fight Killer Phrases; it might be helpful to supplement these methods with some thoughts about how to generate ideas and hold your own in everyday, moment-by-moment situations. In other words, how do you integrate freedom so that you have it in all kinds of circumstances, including those where you don't have the luxury of thinking through these steps or philosophizing about creativity?

Corresponding to every formal method written in this book, there are the quick, informal, intuitive, unwritten ways people have of being creative. These are very personal; I can only give guidelines and examples that will help you recognize those ways that are yours.

To be "ready," in the process of "Ready, Fire . . . Aim!" involves most of all a willingness to unfocus away from what we assume and accept and to refocus in a new way. This means, in day-to-day situations, being willing to give up the safety of straight-line thinking in order to hear yourself think or say the unexpected, the "maybe-this-is-crazy-but-it-just-occurred-to-me" hunch. And, indeed, it *may* strike everyone else as crazy—that's the risk we all take in the name of great ideas, human progress and personal satisfaction!

Refocusing often means opening a side door or back entrance in your mind, so that daydreaming and doodling, for example—or walking or playing music— have a chance to enrich your work. The process of free association requires first, *un*association, then *re*association, letting yourself drift away or detach from those things "we all know" so that maybe you can find something none of us ever thought of. In conversations, conferences, or meetings, it means going with your gut, whatever that means to you. And even though that can also require gutting it out against Killer Phrases, you don't necessarily have to remember a battery of techniques for overcoming them. Your fundamental ally, which can sooner or later overcome any set of killer assumptions, is your faith in your own creative process. In yourself.

The Second Step

EXPRESSION

One step beyond the freedom to consider new possibilities is the ability to give voice to the problems and questions that the new ideas will address. At the beginning of the idea-generating process, you must feel free to say what's wrong or what's wanted—what's going on in this organization—what do we need. Appeal for help: ask questions.

In the following chapters you'll find ways to make certain that your real questions get asked. Question asking, you'll discover, is an art form, with specific techniques required of the truly creative person. The correct ways of expressing those questions are all-important, for on the questions hinge the answers.

Chapter 4

DEAR ABBY
Exploring the Problem

Whoever you are, you have issues and situations in need of creative solutions. Whether you work for a large organization, for a small one, or for yourself—whether you belong to civic clubs or prefer to cultivate your life at home—whether you're married or single—whether you have children or no children, whether you're a student or a professional—you need ideas.

You need great ideas. Ideas to succeed or to maintain a level of success. Ideas to create. To change. To grow. To excel. To have fun. Ideas for business, for school, for term papers, for research projects, for organizational development, for ad campaigns, for product design and development, for educational reform, for effective governmental services.

Ideas for a different, not-to-be-forgotten Christmas present. Ideas for a relaxing weekend with family or friends.

"But where do ideas come from?" you ask. "Don't they just come out of the blue? Doesn't inspiration strike like some unsummoned bolt of lightning? Can I actually control the creation of ideas?"

> **CREATIVE RULE OF THUMB #7**
>
> **The answer to any problem "pre-exists." We need to ask the right question to reveal the answer.**
> —Jonas Salk[1]

Ideas come from you; they are not unsummoned; and you already control the creation of your ideas.

Ideas sometimes do seem to come from out of the blue. But only after you've been ruminating about a problem, a situation, a crisis, or a plan. Rarely does an idea unrelated to you or your surroundings just pop

---

1. *A World of Ideas with Bill Moyers*, "The Science of Hope with Jonas Salk," PBS Video, 1990.

into your head. Instead, it comes for a reason. Often that reason is a needed solution to a very real problem.

The habit of generating those ideas can be developed, as you're now learning.

First, the Problem

Before you can have ideas to solve a problem, you must know what your problem is. Sure, that's obvious, but you'd be surprised at the number of people who have trouble articulating what the problem is. And, of course, not everyone views a given situation in the same way. Some might look at a situation and not see any problems at all.

The first requirement, then, is "Problem Articulation." As in any other phase of the creative process, there are creative ways to do this.

Problem Articulation

In my workshops, I have participants try a relatively simple step-by-step process to formulate problems. The process relies on "Ready, Fire . . . Aim!" thinking to state what the problem is. It also seeks new perspectives by having you look at the problem from the viewpoints of other people affected by it.

To assist you in articulating problems, I've prepared the Problem Articulation Action Sheet (page 51). People in business or government can use it as the broad outline of a report or plan; students may use the approach as beginning mental steps when preparing a paper or dissertation.

Before you start using this Action Sheet, you need to know something about Idea Mapping.[2] Idea Mapping is a fast, five-minute exercise in word and idea association; it relies on keywords, colors, and graphics to form a nonlinear network of potential ideas and observations. It leads to spontaneous idea generation and a vast amount of visible information.

To show you what an Idea Map looks like, I've prepared an Idea Map on . . . why not . . . the potential uses of Idea Maps.

---

2. Idea Mapping was called Mind Mapping by its inventor, Tony Buzan. Now in schools around the world it's also called Idea Mapping, Clustering, Webbing, and Spidering. Thank you, Tony, for a Great Idea!

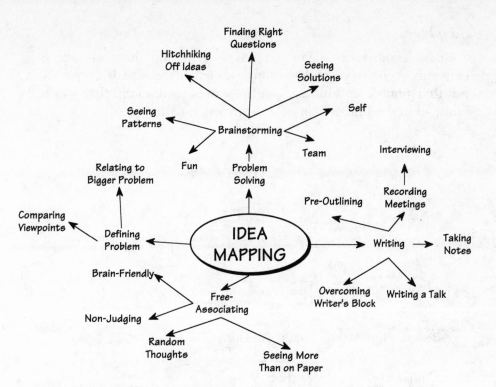

To create an Idea Map, I follow these steps:

Step One

State the problem [READY].

Step Two

Write in the center of your sheet a word or phrase that describes the essence of your problem and put a circle around it. Let's call that word the Trigger Word [READY].

Step Three

Now, without judging, fire away for two minutes and write down around this Trigger Word as many aspects of your problem as you can think of. Do not evaluate their quality; just keep firing [FIRE].

Step Four

See if any of the words are related to any of the others. If so, draw arrows between them, connecting your key thoughts. Build up as many associations as you like. Add more words as necessary [FIRE].

Step Five

Step back and look at your entire map to find three or four main concepts. Assign a geometric symbol to each of those main concepts and put that symbol around each of the words in the map that would be grouped under that concept. This process is called "clustering" [AIM].

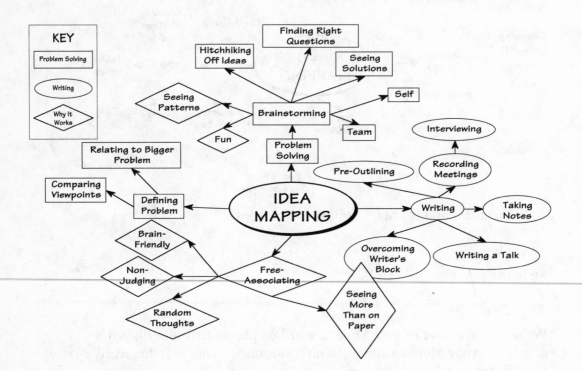

Step Six

Now create a cluster outline. Put the three or four geometric symbols with main concepts written inside at the top of another sheet of paper. Then list the related words from the map below each symbol. Rank in an order that seems logical to you [AIM]. A cluster outline for our Idea Map is shown at the top of the next page.

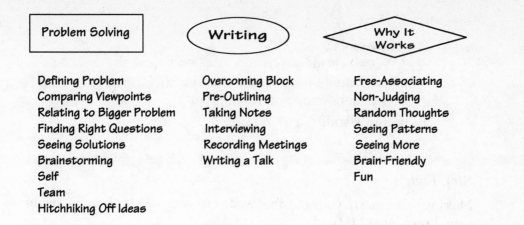

Problem Solving	Writing	Why It Works
Defining Problem	Overcoming Block	Free-Associating
Comparing Viewpoints	Pre-Outlining	Non-Judging
Relating to Bigger Problem	Taking Notes	Random Thoughts
Finding Right Questions	Interviewing	Seeing Patterns
Seeing Solutions	Recording Meetings	Seeing More
Brainstorming	Writing a Talk	Brain-Friendly
Self		Fun
Team		
Hitchhiking Off Ideas		

Step Seven

If you desire a linear outline, transcribe your Idea Map into an outline by using the main concept words for "Roman-numeral" entries and the other words for "A, B, C," "1, 2, 3," and so on [AIM].

The resulting linear outline of Idea Mapping looks like this:

I. Problem Solving

    A. Defining Problem
        1. Comparing different viewpoints
        2. Relating to the bigger problem
        3. Finding right questions to ask

    B. Seeing Solutions
        1. Brainstorming
            a. Self
            b. Team
        2. Hitchhiking from other solutions

II. Writing

    A. Overcoming Writer's Block
        1. Report writing
        2. Writing talks

    B. Pre-outline Technique
        1. Taking notes
        2. Recording lectures
        3. Interviewing

III. Why It Works
   A. Free Association
      1. Suspends judgment
      2. Disjointed thoughts, then arranged
      3. See more than is written down
   B. Brain-Friendly
   C. Fun

Step Eight

Making reference to your outline, write out suggested solutions to your stated problem (AIM).

For example, based on the entry for Roman numeral I, A, you might write:

> *"Idea Maps facilitate problem solving by helping to define the problem. They place different viewpoints about the problem side by side in a graphic relationship, which helps us see the questions we need to ask."*

Discovering the Target

To borrow from our discussion of "Ready . . . Fire . . . Aim!" in Chapter 2, you can see that you're firing off as many words as you can, hoping you'll hit something. *After* firing, look at your Idea Map to see whether you scored any worthwhile relationships between words. The relational patterns and concepts will jump out at you and will be sources of ideas.

Problem Articulation

On another sheet of paper, answer the questions and complete the exercises below.

Step 1 Write a tentative problem statement. Without thinking in detail about the problem, record your initial impressions. Focus on central issues at this point; don't worry now about causes or cures.

Step 2 Explore your problem with an Idea Map. Write a Trigger Word describing the essence of your problem in a center circle. Then write down as quickly as you can words associated with your Trigger Word; put these words all around the center circle. Look for new associations. Draw arrows from one word to another connecting your key thoughts. Add more words as necessary.

Step 3 Look for the main concepts and patterns in your Idea Map. Assign geometric symbols to your main concepts and "cluster" your words by putting the respective symbol around each related word.

Step 4 Create an outline. Now transcribe your Idea Map into either a cluster or Roman-numeral outline.

Step 5 Further clarify the problem. This exercise will help you clarify the views of those people most concerned with how the problem is solved, e.g., the "stakeholders" of the problem. The key question to ask is "Do the other major stakeholders in this problem have different points of view and why?"

	Stakeholder	Point of View	Why?
1.			
2.			
3.			

Step 6 Restate your problem. Looking carefully at your problem outline and incorporating different points of view, now write a carefully worded description of the precise problem needing great ideas for its solution.

"Dear Abby"

In my creativity seminars, I encourage participants to write a "Dear Abby" letter describing a problem needing either their organization's or their own attention. The technique works wonders.

The letter, I point out, should read just like a "Dear Abby" letter you find in the newspaper. It should state what the problem is and should include as many examples of the problem as possible.

This device also works well in meetings. When faced with a troublesome problem (better communication in the office, a need to penetrate new markets, problems with a current ad agency), you should get everyone who is involved with that problem together and announce that they have thirty minutes to write a publishable "Dear Abby" letter. The "Dear Abby" letters you get back from the group will serve as the first step in articulating the exact problem or goal you want to tackle.

An executive in one of my workshops was concerned about poor communication in his organization. His letter looked like this:

Dear Abby,

We just aren't communicating effectively anymore. I'm sure that I'm the problem because I always seem to be in meetings and little seems to be getting done. Maybe I'm too secretive. Maybe my door is closed too often. Maybe I just don't provide the right kind of information to the right people at the right time. Speaking of "right," the right hand doesn't know what the left hand is doing. If a policy is made, it either isn't being communicated or, worse, is being ignored. Rapid growth seems to be playing a part, for many new employees are joining the division. Abby, can you give me some advice?

Signed,
Losing Touch in Atlanta

Q & A

Writing a "Dear Abby" not only helps you ask the question that needs asking but once written puts you and your colleagues in the role of Abby, one of the greatest question answerers of all time. As we'll explore further, question asking and answering are art forms that produce great ideas.

Idea Mapping for Solutions

According to Yoshiro NakaMats, a way to facilitate the creation of ideas is to allow your thoughts about a problem to flow freely before you begin research or talk about it to others. By allowing your thoughts to flow untainted, you build a foundation of how you feel about the problem; you stay close to your original vision or impulse, and you get a record of it. This is contrary to the way many of us were taught, which was to start research or interview experts before we even formed an opinion.

Idea Mapping is an excellent tool for the downloading of these original thoughts. Just prior to brainstorming in a meeting, I recommend that everyone do an individual Idea Map about the problem we're going to discuss; this way their own thoughts are recorded and not lost to the group's brainstorming. The individual maps also provide an excellent warm-up for the brainstorming session.

Let's see how Idea Maps work in a real situation. As an example, suppose your company or division suffers from poor morale. Everybody's down in the dumps, no one seems energized or inspired.

You decide to use an Idea Map to bring out as many aspects of the current situation as possible. Here is what your Idea Map might look like, based on "Poor Morale":

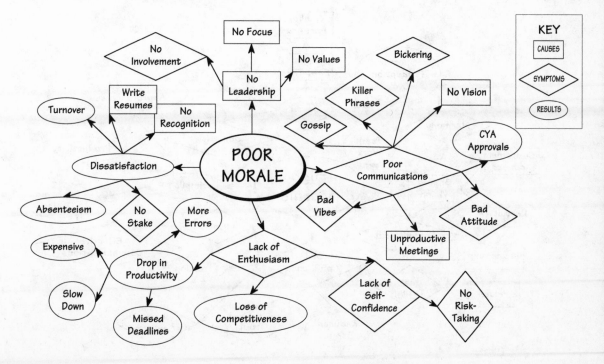

That's Just the Beginning

The example of "Ready, Fire . . . Aim!" Idea Mapping we've just done could help us produce a number of good ideas. However, let's assume that you're not sure how the various elements are linked with each other. What can seem to be a cause might really be a symptom of the problem, and you have to look deeper for the root cause.

To reach a more refined understanding of your problems and opportunities, you can vary your Trigger Word to produce new Idea Maps until you can see your priorities clearly. I recommend varying the Trigger Word in three ways: Trigger Word "When Solved," or the desired future situation; Trigger Word "Comes from," or the problem's roots in the past; and at least one Idea Map with a special twist designed to uncover further ideas that are both unexpected and very specific. For this purpose we choose among Idea Maps with 1) a Metaphorical Trigger Word, 2) an Opposite Trigger Word, or 3) a Random Trigger Word.

Trigger Word "When Solved . . ."

Here we use a problem-solving approach discussed in detail in Chapter 6. We envision the desired situation—high morale—as if it were accom-

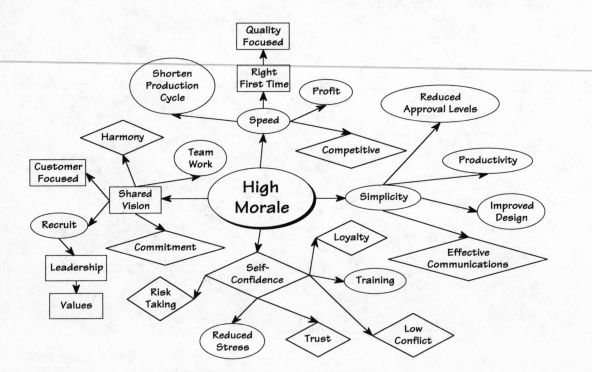

plished and we were there right now. What's our company or unit like
with high morale? What does that tell us—what can we infer from this
picture—about the steps that got us there?

"The steps that got us there" could very well give you all the ideas
you need. But let's save those for our final outline and build an even
greater store of ideas by moving on to:

Trigger Word "Comes from . . ."

Get to the problem's roots by adding "comes from" after your Trigger
Word. Using "Poor Morale" again, we produce the Idea Map below.

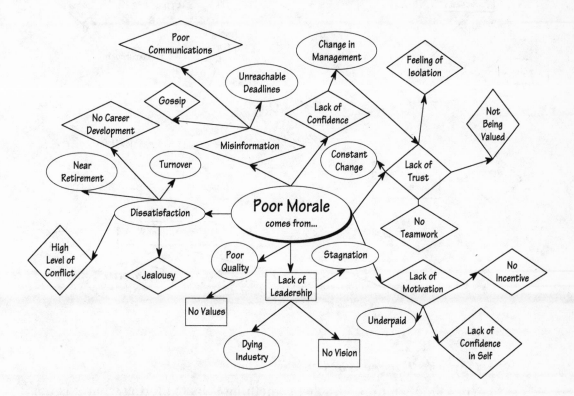

By now you see that your company's outcomes follow from the
identified symptoms, which are a result of the underlying causes. These
insights could lead you to some great-idea leaps. However, you may not
have as many ideas as you'd like for addressing the problem in a creative
way. That's why I like to do one map that "reframes" the problem. For
demonstration purposes, we'll do three different kinds.

Metaphorical Trigger Word

To gain a different perspective on your problem, couch it in metaphorical terms. By seeing related metaphors or similes, you can often come up with unique solutions.

Poor morale in an organization is like . . . a rainy day! Using "rainy day," we can produce the Idea Map below.

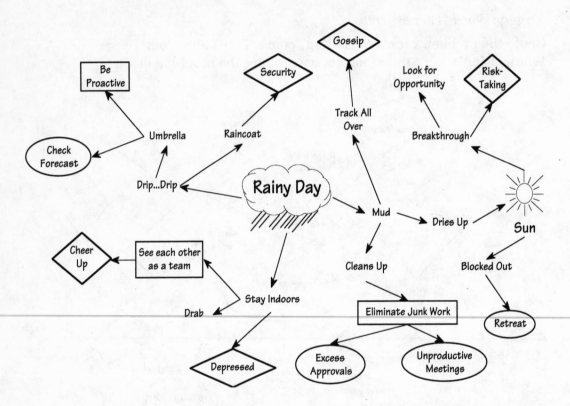

Opposite Trigger Word

You can often find out what something is by exploring what it is not. Instead of putting your problem in the Idea Map as the Trigger Word, write down its exact opposite. The opposite of *poor morale*, of course, is *enthusiasm*. Using it as the Trigger Word, we can produce the Idea Map on the next page.

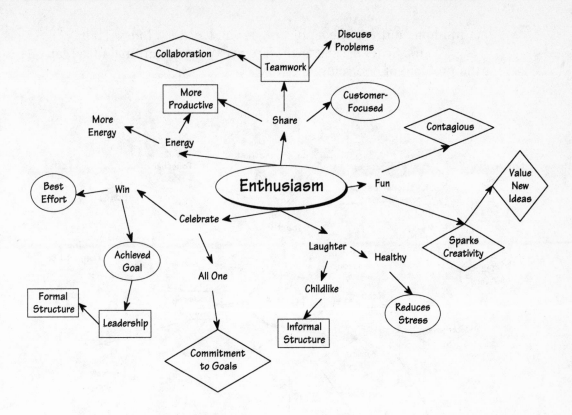

Random Trigger Word

Finally, to give you yet another perspective on your problem, use an absolutely random Trigger Word in your Idea Map. Use any word at all. Go to the dictionary, pick a page at random, and blindly point to a word on the page. Use that word as a Trigger Word. If a dictionary isn't handy or if you need to ruminate on a problem, take a hike. Literally. Go for a walk around the block or a stroll through the park. The first thing that catches your eye . . . use that as a Trigger Word. If you need encouragement, consider the experience of Knute Rockne, the famous Notre Dame football coach. "I got my idea for my 'four horsemen backfield shift,'" he said, "while watching a burlesque chorus routine."

    Let's see it work. As I'm writing this book I am now turning away from my computer keyboard toward my telephone. I'm picking up my copy of the yellow pages and wondering whether readers will really believe that the word I pick was chosen completely by chance. Whatever the word is, I hope it doesn't look too easy. Okay, I'm turning to a page at random, and, let's see, pointing to the word . . . *tours*. Tours?

Tours. So let's use it as the Trigger Word in our final Idea Map on the problem of poor morale.

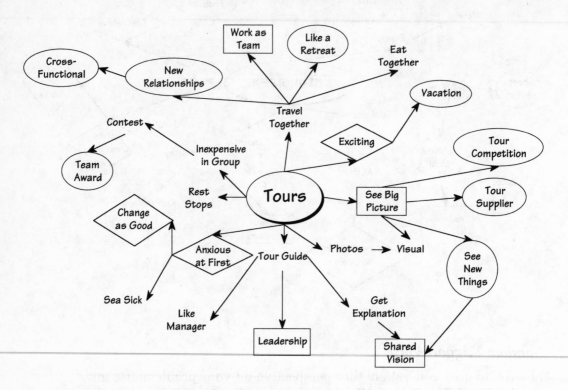

Comparing Your Idea Maps

For "Poor Morale" we've generated key concepts related to everything from "Where it comes from" to "What it is not." To synthesize your Idea Maps, you can put them side by side on a table or tape them to a wall. Then step back and see if you notice any associations from one map to another.

On looking at the collected Idea Maps on poor morale, you can make an outline of all the thoughts and associations. This outline can be ordered by immediacy of action or just by definition of the problem from general to specific.

The following outline is my analysis of the problem of poor morale as taken from the six Idea Maps.

I. Factors Affecting Organizational Morale

    A. Causes

    B. Symptoms

    C. Results

II. Variábles

    A. Causal variables
        1. Lack of leadership
        2. Values not followed
        3. No shared vision
        4. No focus on customer
        5. Constant change
        6. Don't see organization as a whole

    B. Intervening variables
        1. Commitment to organization
        2. No risk-taking
        3. Poor communications
        4. High level of conflict
        5. Gossip
        6. Lack of confidence
        7. No teamwork
        8. Lack of trust
        9. No incentive

    C. Outcome Variables
        1. Poor quality
        2. Customer complaints
        3. Decreasing productivity
            a. Slowdown
            b. More errors
        4. Lack of competitiveness
        5. Missed goals and deadlines
        6. Falling profit and ROI
        7. Job dissatisfaction
            a. Turnover
            b. Absenteeism
            c. Underpaid
        8. More C.Y.A. approvals
        9. Constant management changes
     10. Act like dying industry

III. Action Recommendations

A. Create a vision
   1. Make it understandable
   2. Make it inspiring
   3. Include in performance appraisals

B. Encourage collaboration
   1. Set up project work teams
   2. Knock down hierarchical and divisional walls
   3. Foster an environment for creativity and risk-taking
   4. Measure and reward team efforts
   5. Hold offsite retreats
   6. Initiate cross-functional training

C. Take a customer-focused orientation
   1. Understand external customer
   2. Understand internal customer
   3. Identify customer needs
   4. Measure and reward customer satisfaction

D. Initiate a continuous improvement process
   1. Eliminate unnecessary junk work
      a. Reports
      b. Approvals
      c. Meetings
      d. Measurements
      e. Policies
   2. Work as cross-functional teams to find better ways
   3. Include customers and suppliers in process

You can also convert the outline back into a graphic representation, to show important relationships—as shown below.

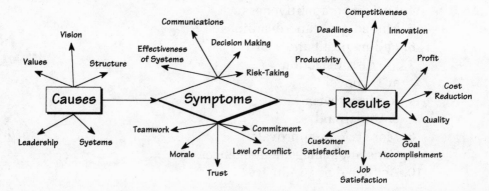

Uses of Idea Maps

You can expand the uses of Idea Mapping to cover a host of situations and to serve as a catalyst for positive organizational change. Consider the following variations of Idea Mapping.

Idea Maps and Report Writing

At my creativity workshops, many participants ask about the actual "use" of Idea Maps. They can see how word association helps the creative process, but they also want to see how Idea Maps might function within an organization or help them complete a task. Over the years, I've stressed that Idea Maps are ideal exercises for preparing written analyses of problems, strategies, plans, and programs.

The key lies in the notion of "synthesis." Idea Maps produce a flood of words, unrelated words, concrete words, words that seemingly bear little relationship to one another. But when the Idea-Mapping process is over, you can look at the words you've produced and synthesize them into larger conceptual groupings. And when you're looking at a series of Idea Maps, the larger conceptual groupings might merge into even larger groupings. These larger groupings, when appropriately labeled, then serve as the "organizational milestones" for a written report. They serve, if you will, as the Roman numerals in a broad outline of your problem.

A colleague of mine teaches persuasive writing courses to law firms, government agencies, and corporations. Recently he began to teach Idea Mapping as a device for organizing and brainstorming topics for written papers. At one recent course, a student raised her hand and said, "This Idea Mapping is similar to the 'front cover/back cover' approach to exam taking we used at Harvard. When I was a freshman, a professor told me to brainstorm on the inside front cover of the exam blue book and to outline on the inside back cover of the blue book. That way, professors could see that I'd covered the main topics even if time ran out on the exam!"

Indeed, the approach is similar. The front-cover brainstorming is the Idea Mapping. The back-cover outlining is identical to the synthesis you use to name and organize your thoughts.

Comparison Mapping

If your task is to synergize the views of various stakeholders, you can create a multicentered Idea Map with one Trigger Word and position other centered Trigger Words derived from different stakeholders. It might look like the one below.

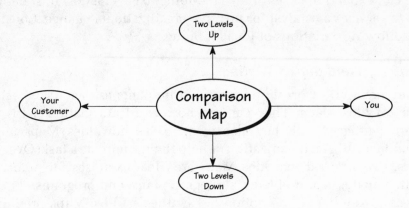

Then fire away with words from each new stakeholder's perspective. Look for interrelationships, draw connecting arrows, and put geometric symbols around any common elements you spot.

By the way, it sometimes reduces the pressure in a problem-solving session if you define your more conventional options or solutions first. As one ad agency's creative director said, "We start with what we call 'The Save'—a safe solution to the problem we know the client and the account group can agree with. It's not necessarily noncreative, but it's safe. That takes a burden off our shoulders. Then we can let go and look for the big 'aha,' something that's never been done before" (Norins, *The Young & Rubicam Traveling Creative Workshop*).

Team Mapping

Use Idea Maps on flip charts as a means of eliciting ideas from a group in a meeting. Group Idea Mapping can be a key technique for engendering true collaboration in the organization, as we'll explore further in Chapter 16. In *Shared Minds: The New Technologies of Collaboration* (New York: Random House, 1990), Michael Schrage notes that even though the blackboard or whiteboard is "the most pervasive of collaborative media," indispensable in labs and universities, they are almost never found in a business office—a sign of the isolation in which many of us work. Team mapping and the two variations on Idea Mapping that follow can help fill an organization's need for interpersonal media to create ideas. These techniques can also pave the way for groups and teams to learn how to collaborate via a shared computer screen.

Vision Mapping

On a large marker board, put your goal as the Trigger Word in the center of an Idea Map, surround it with empty circles, hang it for all to see, and challenge yourselves to fill up the circles with actions that will have to take place to achieve the goal.

The Living Map

Create an ongoing Idea Map to elicit suggestions from staff or department heads. Position the Living Idea Map in high-traffic areas such as break areas, cafeterias, and exercise rooms. Alternate by department the responsibility of writing down the "Trigger Word of the Month."

The Graphics Map

Create a colorful Idea Map using graphics, cartoons, symbols, and very few words. I almost always use colors in my Idea Maps in any case. Using a multicolored Bic pen or Crayola crayons, I start with one color for the Trigger Word, another color for the words around it, another color for the arrows between them, and additional colors for the geometric symbols.

Incidentally, the need for people to be free and spontaneous—and fast—in their Idea Mapping means that I often suggest they do it in their native language, even if I'm working in the United States or another country where most of the participants speak English. After one session, in the U.S., a woman came up to me and said, "You know, as soon as you asked us to Idea Map I started writing down all my words in German—and I haven't written in German in fifteen years!" The process itself brought out her most natural response.

People often ask me why they have to put words all over the page and then try to link words that are out at the edges of the paper, seemingly scattered and unrelated. I recently read something which sums it up rather nicely: "At the boundary, life blossoms" (James Gleick, *Chaos: Making a New Science* [New York: Viking-Penguin, 1987]).

Spontaneous Idea Maps

Idea Maps are an excellent vehicle for quick, unstructured self-brainstorming sessions when you need help with a variety of everyday problems. Use a legal pad, for example, turned sideways (so that you don't work top to bottom). Or make maps on a napkin or a placemat at a restaurant or cafeteria. Instead of making your usual, linear to-do list,

Idea Map it, and you'll be surprised by the results.

I've used all of these methods and find that the common requirement for remembering or storing the generated information is to make sure that you transcribe all Idea Maps into an outline or ordered list.

Seeing the Future with an Idea Map

Idea Mapping provides a workable way for combining bits of information that will shape the future. It graphically allows you to see how the pieces are going to fit together in areas as diverse as consumer tastes, interest rates, health care costs, and property taxes.

Many firms now offer trend-spotting services to companies and government agencies. The most prominent of these firms is Inferential Focus, a consulting group that doesn't draw bar charts to show predicted trends: they create Idea Maps from observations culled from more than three hundred newspapers, trade papers, and technical magazines. They look for "anomalies" and then infer their meaning. "Change always occurs outside of where you're looking for it," explains principal Carol Colman. The secret to inferring business trends is to "read voraciously, eliminate opinion, try to draw connections between events, and adhere to the 'three or five' rule." The "three or five" rule means waiting to get three or five confirmations of something you suspect, all from different sources. These sources can be interrelated on Idea Maps.

Suggested Trigger Words

Although you undoubtedly have scores of Trigger Words defining a host of problems, here's a proven list of Trigger Words that I guarantee will generate great ideas for you:

Closer to Customer	*Higher Quality*
Improve Communications	*Zero Defects*
Immediacy	*Reduce Stress*
Automate	*Cut Paperwork*
Meaningful Incentive	*Increase Sales*
Speed Up	*Self-Confidence*
More Profit	*Lower Costs*

Idea Mapping Guide

Take out two sheets of paper—one for stating your problem and recording selected ideas and the other for Idea Mapping. Make sure to have the Idea Mapping sheet turned sideways so that you don't work from the top down.

Step 1 State your problem on first sheet of paper.

Step 2 Choose a Trigger Word.

Note: For Metaphorical, Opposite Word, or Random Word Idea Maps, complete this step by choosing a Trigger Word that serves as a metaphor for your original Trigger Word, the opposite of your original Trigger Word, or a word at random, with no apparent relationship to your original Trigger Word.

Step 3 Idea Map your Trigger Word on second sheet of paper turned sideways.

Write the Trigger Word (or Metaphorical, Opposite, or Random Trigger Word) in the center circle. Then write down as quickly as you can words associated with the Trigger Word; put these words all around the center circle. Look for new associations. Draw arrows from one word to another connecting your key thoughts; add more words as necessary.

Step 4 Look for the main concepts and patterns in your Idea Map.

Assign geometric symbols to your main concepts and "cluster" your words by putting the respective symbol around each related word.

Step 5 Create an Idea Outline on first sheet of paper.

Now transcribe your map into either a "cluster" or a Roman-numeral outline.

Step 6 Record your ideas.

Select four ideas that can help you solve the problem.

Software for Words and Ideas

There's a boom in computer software to help you reframe your problem and free-associate word pairings. The best part of the programs is that they can automatically generate outlines from your Idea Mapping.

The best Idea-Mapping software at this writing is called Inspiration (see "Resources"). I used Inspiration to do the maps in this book; it's an excellent tool that permits you to create your map almost instantly as the elements occur to you. Inspiration creates the rectangles, ovals—and even clouds—that hold your words even as you write them, and lays out arrows connecting the elements as you move from word to word.

It's really true, as Inspiration's makers claim, that its "rapid-fire quick entry captures a surge of ideas as fast as you can think of them"—and does so in a flexible way, so that symbols grow automatically to fit text, symbols can be rearranged, unconnected thoughts added, and so on. These aspects of Inspiration alone would make it a wonderful software both for Idea Mapping and for creating presentations. But Inspiration also automatically generates an outline from the Idea Map, and the outline can in turn be edited and rearranged.

At the moment, the most powerful idea-generation software overall is IdeaFisher, which does not involve Idea Mapping. Marsh Fisher, cofounder of the real estate giant Century 21 International, retired in 1977 to play golf and to understand better the creative thinking process. Twelve years and $4 million later, IdeaFisher was released.

IdeaFisher, a computerized aid to brainstorming and problem-solving, helps speed up the creative process. Marsh came to the class that I teach at the Federal Executive Institute to demonstrate his software—and it was amazing. I bought a copy for my Macintosh on the spot; it's also available for IBM-compatible PCs.

IdeaFisher consists of an interactive database of questions and idea words and phrases. Questions are organized to help you define, clarify, modify, and evaluate your needs. You can even add your own questions to the three thousand already supplied. More than sixty thousand idea words and phrases are structured in 28 major categories and 387 topical categories. This puts more than seven hundred thousand direct idea associations at your fingertips.

Described by one reviewer as "a giant library with many doorways," IdeaFisher can give you easily more than one thousand associations, grouped in categories, for a single word—let's say the key word in the topic of your next report or talk. Store the ideas you want to play with on the program's notepad, add your own notes to them via the text editor, then print or transfer to another program such as word processing.

Knowledge workers who issue reports, plans, designs, briefs, scripts, and projections in some of the largest companies in the world are now using the program. So are marketing professionals, lawyers, design engineers, ad executives, television and movie producers, and others whose jobs involve strategy, planning, consulting, or marketing. I've used IdeaFisher to develop scripts, create metaphors, and develop a promotional campaign along with slogans.

Fisher states that creating ideas is "a process, not an accident. You plant, you fertilize, you harvest." With IdeaFisher plus the techniques you're learning here, I'm sure you'll raise a bumper crop.

> *Idea-generation software helps you reframe your problem by allowing you to draw Idea Maps or by generating new idea words from your keywords.*

Inspiration and IdeaFisher are among the "thinking tools" that Paul Anakar of *PCAI Magazine* calls "the next computer revolution." The ones I've described are among the "creativity enhancement" programs. Another type is "hyperlinking" software, which allows you to enrich what would be a linear presentation with related tangential thoughts and associations. Side thoughts, details that helped you formulate your ideas, examples, and so on can be placed and accessed behind the main flow of the material. "Decision analysis," another emerging tool, can help people uncover and consider, among other things, previously unknown factors affecting their choices. "Real world simulation," while obviously a good way to train and develop skills for a given situation, can also promote creativity. "Because there are no dire consequences from making mistakes," Anakar says, "the user has the freedom to be more creative. That can lead to being more creative in real life" (Paul Anakar, "Thinking Tools: The Next Computer Movement," *The Mindware Catalog* [Santa Cruz, Calif.: The Mindware Review, 1991]).

Several of the new idea-generation programs on the market are listed in the Resources section of this book.

Chapter 5

DUMB QUESTIONS
Forerunners to Innovation

Questions invite innovation. A question posed to the right person on the right topic at the right time can hand you keys to a wealth of information and ideas. People love to talk. You can instill creativity in yourself by getting them to talk to you.

If you'd like proof that questions are powerful instruments, try a little experiment, which in itself can spark valuable ideas. Find someone and ask, "If you had three wishes right now, what would they be?" Stand back and watch what happens.

Questions ask for talk. Statements require passive listening. The creative manager won't approach a division chief and make the statement, "This department is failing." The astute manager will *pose the question*: "If you were me, what could we do to change things around here?"

To Find the Answer, Ask the Question

If you're seeking great ideas, the first step is often asking great questions, because the way you look at a problem can dictate how you seek its solution. Thomas MacAvoy, former president and chief operating officer of Corning Glass Works, for example, relates the most creative question ever asked in his professional life. One day, while MacAvoy was a senior chemist in a lab at Corning, Corning's president said to the head of research, "Glass breaks. Why don't you do something about that?" The directive to the lab then became: "We're going to prevent glass from breaking." The lab came up with twenty-five different ways of preventing glass from breaking; eighteen of them worked, and five made money.

The most interesting aspect of this exchange is not what the president did ask but what he *did not ask*. He did not ask "Why does glass break?" That question might have produced months of exhaustive research, resulting in some highly scientific reports, which would collect dust on a shelf. Instead, the boss went straight for the desired solution: How can we make glass that doesn't break? The end result was the now-famous Corelle line of dinnerware.

As a consultant commissioned to train General Electric personnel in the new GE "Work-Out!" mind-set, designed to instill speed, simplicity, and self-confidence in the workplace, I was challenged to come up with the right questions for workshop participants. "Work-Out!" was designed to speed up GE operations, but instead of asking, "How can you speed up your operations?" I asked, "How can you accomplish your work in half the time?" This led everyone to search for new ways to do specific tasks and not merely step on the gas in an effort to do the same old things faster.

The Vision-Driven Question

What the Corning and GE examples show is rather simply stated. Focus on the desired vision and frame a concrete question around it. Other examples of the technique abound in industry. When I interviewed the developer of Jiffy Lube, he told me he had asked, "How can we give a ten-minute oil and lube job?" Not "How can we speed up car servicing?" After moving from a thirty-day to a fifteen-day mortgage approval, Citicorp asked, "How can we approve a home mortgage in fifteen minutes?" Not "How can we improve our mortgage service?" or "How can we attract more home mortgage customers?" Citicorp increased its home mortgage business more than 100 percent in one year in an industry with a 3 percent growth rate. Is fifteen minutes too fast to provide adequate background checks? Probably, for some, and that's where learning and self-correcting from small failures comes in as a safety net.

Asking for Second Right Answers

Ever since we started school, we've been trained to look for "the right answer." Think of all those multiple-choice exams where each question had just one right answer. We've been conditioned to seek the one and only answer. Breaking that habit won't be easy, so I recommend staying away from "We've got to find *the* solution" and instead easing into a new frame of mind by saying, "We need to look at some possible solutions to this problem." Although the difference might seem like word playing, it really is developing a new perspective—an inquisitive perspective that seeks a host of ideas by asking a host of questions in search of a host of potential solutions.

> *One day the president of Corning Glass said to the head of research, "Glass breaks. Why don't you do something about that?"*

To that end, I often advise participants in problem-solving workshops and meetings to think of two words when formulating their questions: *flexible* and *focused*. When writing out your question, make it flexible so that it's open to other people's interpretations and views of other "stakeholders" in the organization—and make it focused, so that you'll know when the answers you get satisfy your question.

Asking Dumb Questions

Tom Peters in *Thriving on Chaos: Handbook for a Management Revolution* (New York: Alfred A. Knopf, 1987) emphasizes the power of the dumb question. In his words,

> *Mostly, it's the dumb, elementary questions followed up by a dozen even more elementary questions that yield the pay dirt. Experts are those who don't need to bother with elementary questions anymore—thus they fail to bother with the true sources of bottlenecks buried deep in habitual routines of the firm labeled "We've always done it that way."*

As Helgesen pointed out in *The Female Advantage: Women's Ways of Leadership*, many successful executives nurture a streak of craziness in themselves, a trait they view as necessary to asking "dumb," but penetrating, questions. According to Nancy Badore, a top-level Ford executive in charge of managerial training,

> *Being crazy means I let myself ask even really stupid questions. And I have to do that, because it's something I try to encourage around this place. When executives come in for the training programs, they're often reluctant to ask questions or challenge*

speakers, because they don't want to look like idiots. If we want to get them talking up the ladder—sharing their ideas, not being afraid—we've got to get them past all that. One thing I can do is use myself as an example. They see I'm not afraid to look ridiculous, and that helps to set the tone (Helgesen, The Female Advantage).

Suggested Dumb Questions

1. Why have we always done it that way?

2. Does anyone actually look at that form?

3. Why do I have to sign this form?

4. Why can't I send a handwritten letter?

5. Why do I need a hard copy of this report?

6. Why do we need a committee to look into this?

7. What's a _____? (fill in the blank with any high-tech term used by a high-tech type)

The Six Universal Questions

Idea Generators should be aware of a simple universal truth: There are only six questions that one human can ask another: What? Where? When? How? Why? Who?

Innovators and Idea Generators can constantly ask the Six Universal Questions as sparks for ideas and solutions to problems. They can even use the Six Universal Questions as a methodical way to tear a problem apart or as an effective way to organize a presentation of a particular problem. They can take each question separately and seek as many answers as they can possibly find. They can use questions to lead to other productive questions.

As an exercise, we can use the Six Universal Questions approach

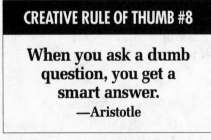

CREATIVE RULE OF THUMB #8

When you ask a dumb question, you get a smart answer.
—Aristotle

as a way of creating some really great questions—as a way to unravel a problem to see its many facets—and as a way of framing our problem so that workable solutions suggest themselves. In the Great Idea Action Sheet on page 75, I've posed six questions about your problem. We'll simply call your problem "it."

Here are the Six Universal Questions about "it." Now fire away!

1. *What is it?*

2. *Where does it happen?*

3. *When does it happen?*

4. *How does it happen?*

5. *Why does it happen?*

6. *To whom does it happen?/ Who causes it to happen?*

The Five Questions "Why"

To get at the root of your problem I suggest you ask yourself why it's occurring, then counter your answer with *why?* four more times. A recent book on the Toyota production system (Yuzo Yasuda, *40 Years, 20 Million Ideas: The Toyota Suggestion System* [Cambridge, Mass.: Productivity Press, 1991]) reveals that Toyota workers are trained to do just this when they confront a problem. For example:

1. Why has the machine stopped?
   A fuse blew because of an overload.
2. Why was there an overload?
   There wasn't enough lubrication for the bearings.
3. Why wasn't there enough lubrication?
   The pump wasn't pumping enough.
4. Why wasn't enough lubricant being pumped?
   The pump shaft was vibrating as a result of abrasion.
5. Why was there abrasion?
   There was no filter, which allowed chips of material to get into the pump.

Installation of a filter solves the problem.

The challenge for one manager with whom I worked was that she never had enough time to finish her to-do list.

1. Why?—
   There are too many unexpected interruptions in my day.
2. Why?—
   I have an open-door policy.
3. Why?—
   I want my staff to have my input when they have a crisis.
4. Why?—
   We work as a team and I can offer many years of experience.
5. Why?—
   Teamwork and sharing make our company productive.

By asking *why* she has found that her interruptions are necessary to make the company and staff productive. She needs to factor interruptions into her to-do list and time management and feel great when her opinion is being sought.

This executive could have gone on indefinitely feeling self-critical and frustrated. If we don't get to the root of the problem it will grow back, just as dandelions do when you only cut off the yellow.

Innocence Pays

Jonas Salk suggests that asking questions is more productive than trying to come up with answers. "Find the right questions. You don't invent the answers, you reveal the answers" (*A World of Ideas with Bill Moyers*, "The Science of Hope with Jonas Salk," PBS Video, 1990).

Asking dumb or "innocent" questions is a form of having the courage to be naive, to ask even when the answer may be obvious to everyone else, to ask simply because it occurs to you. Such questions are vital steps, because only when you feel free to express your own perspective are you ready for the next phase of the idea-generating process, which involves deliberately altering and expanding that perspective.

See through your own eyes first. Then prepare to see through brand-new eyes.

Six Universal Questions

This sheet poses the Six Universal Questions about the problem you've described below. Answer the questions as freely as you can and then combine your thoughts into two Great Questions to help you solve your problem.

Description of problem:

1. What is it?

2. Where does it happen?

3. When does it happen?

4. How does it happen?

5. Why does it happen?

6. Who causes it to happen? / To whom does it happen?

Now, combine your above responses into two Great Questions.

1.

2.

CONCLUSION

Recently I was asked whether I thought it was possible to "institutionalize" the question-asking process involved in *expression* so that people could have a regular way of using it in their personal and organizational lives. "Or," my friend asked, "is that a self-defeating concept?"

Any organization can incorporate the basics of expression and question asking, even if no organization can plot or predict what the questions will be or where they will lead. It's really impossible for such an attempt to be self-defeating; any method that an organization chooses to encourage questions or free expression will tend to lead to progressive change.

Therefore, it's a fine idea for organizations and groups to incorporate the Six Universal Questions, for example, in a formal way, putting them on display, reminding decision makers to take them into account when considering a problem or goal. A checklist of question-asking procedures, which must be covered in coming to a decision, could save organizations and task groups grief and lead to unexpected new approaches for viewing or solving the problem. New ideas then lead to new questions . . . and more new ideas.

The question-asking process is especially powerful when joined to Idea Mapping—because every question can be expanded and answered with the help of an Idea Map, and the answer can then be explored and expanded with another Idea Map. Through Idea Mapping—or any other form of free-associating ideas—question asking translates into positive expression. On the personal level, remember that Idea Mapping can be informal and quick and can work anywhere—five minutes of drawing on a paper napkin. It's a way that questions can lead to unforced, unexpected, multiple answers.

The Third Step

CREATION

Freedom and *expression*, our first two steps, take you to the point of creation itself. Here's the heart of generating great ideas, and here's much of the fun. The most interesting thing about this process of creation, I believe, is how much fun it really is—how positive and effort free it is, when you understand how it works.

For creating great new ideas is not a process of making something out of nothing—it's not a heroic effort to concentrate one's genius on a problem and somehow conquer it through sheer brilliance. If that's the way problem solving seems to you, you're probably working much too hard—and working against yourself.

> **CREATIVE RULE OF THUMB #9**
>
> **Never solve a problem from its original perspective.**

Creation is fun because it's play. It literally is play because it involves, most of all, playing with the elements we're given. Rather than make something out of nothing—diamond icicles out of thin air—we're always making something new out of something given. The play is in taking the ingredients of this world and *re*-creating them—toying with them, imagining new combinations, new forms, new applications. The more fun it becomes for you, the more you're on the track of the highest kind of creative process.

Highly creative people see things differently; their perspective on problems is different from that of most other people. It's different precisely because they have the habit of imaginatively *un*-creating the world and putting it back together in new ways. It's this different way of looking at problems that distinguishes the highly creative person. But if we look at the way we think when we're at our most creative, then we can begin to change our own perspectives and see more things more of the time in a different light. And see solutions previously hidden from view.

Chapter 6

SELF-FULFILLING PROPHECIES

Envisioning the Future

I was playing golf one afternoon with Bob Rotella. A colleague of mine, Bob has made quite a name for himself in sports psychology, coaching some of the world's top professional golfers. I captured many of Bob's ideas with a highly successful audiocassette program, "Golfing Out of Your Mind." Since that time, *Golf Digest* has retained him to write a regular column on the relationship between the mind and success on the fairway, in bunkers, or on the greens.

On this particular afternoon, I'd become very tentative in my putting, invariably failing to reach the hole. After three-putting a hole, I asked for advice.

Bob shared with me a thought he'd used with various PGA champions. "Don't putt until you know you can make it."

"But Bob," I said, "I'll be here all day waiting for that moment."

> **CREATIVE RULE OF THUMB #10**
>
> **Visualize your problem as solved before solving it.**

He laughed. "Just picture yourself as making the putt. You're picturing yourself *missing* the putt. *Make* the putt. Make the putt in your *mind.*"

Of course, I didn't, and still don't, make every putt I attempt. But using Bob's method has helped me recover from a bad hole and par the next one.

For years, successful basketball coaches have used the same technique. They've taught their players to become better shooters by visualizing the ball going *swish* through the net. The perfect jumper, foul shot, or three pointer, it doesn't touch a bit of the rim—only net. The shooter visualizes the result, during the day, at night before sleep, at practice, and especially during a game. Coaches and players have found that this device can dramatically increase shooting percentages.

Managers are finding that the same thing works to help solve problems in business and industry. The device of envisioning a successful future can be one of the most effective sources of ideas. In a time of rapid change, our problems are becoming more vision driven, so that focusing only on present resources very much restricts our possibilities. We need to balance our "thriving on analysis" method of problem solving—where we quantify the last five years and extrapolate—with the information we can gain from visionary techniques.

Whatever your problem or goal, picture it already solved or completed. What does your future world look like? What does the future business or work environment look like? What does the solution look like? What are its features? How did it get there? How did it come into being? What had to take place for the problem to be solved, the goal to be reached?

The visualizer then works back incrementally to the present, to envision the steps taken to produce that image.

Envisioning the future thus breaks down, as a technique, into four steps: (1) identify the problem or goal, (2) fix a solution or achievement date, (3) visualize the problem or goal reached, and (4) come back from the future.

Step One   Identify the problem or goal

I've already discussed the various ways to identify problems or goals in Chapters 4 and 5. You can use the steps in the Problem Articulation process, the Dear Abby approach, the Dumb Question approach, or the Six Universal Questions approach.

Step Two   Fix a solution or achievement date

You need to decide when the problem must be solved or when the goal should be achieved. The problem or goal might be a long-term one such as desirable sales levels to reach in a five-year plan. Or a short-term one such as current problems of organizational miscommunication.

Step Three   Visualize the problem solved or the goal reached

Here's the essence of the approach. Close your eyes and picture what things will be like if—*when*—the problem is solved or the goal is reached.

Just as you might picture a putt made or a basketball shot swished, picture your problem solved or goal achieved. Don't picture "near misses" or "maybes," picture only success. Insisting on a rigid or narrow picture of the future, such as the precise mix of sales in five years or all the steps to be expected of your competitors, is probably self-defeating. Free your thinking by concentrating on the overall picture of the future, seeing your place in it, and then sketching the specific details that make sense in that setting. Describe a complete scenario depicting your organization *now* in the future.

One useful technique is to write a short newspaper article describing the future as the *present*. What's the headline? What are the news media saying *right now* about your organization's performance? Did it make *Eyewitness News*? If so, what did the news anchor say?

Step Four   Come back from the future

The goal of envisioning the future is to return from the future incrementally—one step at a time. Try to picture all the moves you or the organization had to make to reach the result.

Then revisit the past to see where the problem came from in the first place. Maybe it was a great idea back then, but the conditions changed. Just think back to pre-1980: no personal computer, no fax, no telephone with autodialer, no microwave, no CD player, not yet a VCR in virtually every home.

Executives at Apple Computer use this device when deciding on products to introduce in the computer industry. After attending some of my seminars in creativity, new product development managers at Apple have shared with me their "Back from the Future" planning, which is in substance the same as the Envision-the-Future approach to idea making. The Apple executives envision what the industry will be like, what consumers will be demanding, what the competition will be doing. They identify a desirable and reachable goal for Apple's participation in this future computer industry and then work backward, step by step, to the present day, all the while keeping track of the precise steps needed for goal achievement.

The process is a rich breeding ground for ideas. By reframing their problem or goal, the Apple execs gain a perspective unlike what they would normally experience.

A superb example of "Back from the Future" planning is the process initiated by Smith & Hawken, the highly successful mail-order marketers of fine gardening tools, as described by Peter Schwartz in his book *The Art of the Long View* (New York: Doubleday, 1991). Smith & Hawken's managers projected their firm into the future from the late 1970s, when the company was just starting out. They made plans based on three different broad scenarios for the future of the western world's economy. In one scenario, economic growth, consumption, and materialism continued unabated. In another scenario, the world faced economic depression, famine in the Third World, crisis in the environment, and shortages of natural resources. The third scenario projected a basic shift in western culture toward harmony with the environment, consumption of natural foods, and an emphasis on inner growth.

> A garden tool company prepared for three different futures—and found that all three happened at once.

The next task facing Smith & Hawken was to project the impact of these scenarios on the garden tool market. In the first scenario, gardening would be popular as a status symbol for the affluent—"beautiful gardens" for "beautiful homes." The growing affluent class would have no problem buying the beautifully made, high-quality, relatively expensive tools offered by Smith & Hawken. Under the second projection, gardening would be necessary for survival. The company's products would be in demand because people would need tools that could stand up to heavy use. In the third scenario, "many affluent people would take up pleasant, ecology-conscious hobbies." Gardening would be popular as a meditative activity that promoted inner growth as well as the growth of food and flowers.

Each scenario projected a strong market for garden tools. The next step was to determine how the different possible markets might affect marketing strategy. Under all three projections the planners decided that mail order was preferable to distribution through retail outlets, for Smith & Hawken's special products. In the first case, affluent consumers would be too busy to shop in stores; in the second, stores would tend to have problems surviving; and in the third, mail-order selling would appeal to the "*Whole Earth Catalog*–oriented" type of consumer.

As it turned out, all three scenarios emerged in the 1980s. Yuppies, a large segment of struggling, working poor, and "New Agers" all lived side by side, so that each of the projections was somewhat correct. Smith & Hawken went from $200,000 in sales in its first year to $1 million within three years to recent sales of about $50 million a year.

Management consultant David Israel-Rosen suggests another way for companies to envision the future—by talking to their "lead users." Lead users are the consumers who "live in the future"—and who have come up with uses and modifications of your product that you haven't even considered. Find out what your lead users are doing, Israel-Rosen says, "then walk back to the average users, and ask how they like your new product idea. Are they inclined to follow your lead users? If not, you haven't identified the real lead users, and must start over" (Duncan M. Anderson, "Seize the Future Now!" *Success*, October 1990).

An Example

Let's pause and see how the Envision-the-Future approach has worked for one of my clients. In August 1990 I was asked to lecture in South Africa for the University of South Africa School of Business Leadership. One of their client companies, Protea Insurance, wanted to project the demographic changes that would occur in its market over the next five years. So we used the Envision-the-Future technique.

Step One   Identify the problem

The stated goal was to anticipate what major demographic changes would have the greatest impact on the country's insurance industry by 1995.

Step Two   Establish a solution date

The long-term date was five years.

Step Three   Visit the future and visualize

I instructed the forty-five insurance executives to close their eyes, fast-forward their thoughts to August 20, 1995, and scan a current newspaper, trade magazine, or TV show. They were to see with their mind's eye what the headlines, trends, and patterns were.

Step Four   Come back from the future

After five minutes they opened their eyes and in groups of five I gave them the task of putting together their company newsletter. They were to establish headlines, lead stories, and items of interest such as personnel promotions, retirements, profitability figures, new markets, and so on.

The teams then presented their newsletter mock-ups to the group as a whole and we collected and rank ordered their news items. This information was later incorporated into a report on what's ahead for the insurance industry in South Africa.

To help you along, I've prepared another Great Idea Action Sheet at the end of this chapter. You'll find that it's extremely useful to pass out at meetings when you need other people to come up with some great ideas.

Is What You See What You Get?

I gained an interesting perspective on the Envision-the-Future approach recently from Joe McMoneagle, consultant for Stanford Research Institute in California and the Monroe Institute in Virginia and widely considered one of America's most reliable "remote viewers." "Remote viewer," McMoneagle observes, "is a nice way of saying 'a psychic'"—in this case a psychic who works under strict scientific protocols and who has been the subject in many published experiments. McMoneagle also looks into the future for private and corporate clients.

> *There may be a direct link between how we see the future and how it will in fact be.*

A remote viewer has demonstrated the ability to see things, places, and events removed in time or space. Regardless of one's beliefs about such abilities, McMoneagle's ideas mesh with our emerging common sense about visionary techniques and illuminate the process by which we all go about trying to create a better future. Almost any of his statements can be taken either literally or metaphorically, with similar results.

For example, McMoneagle thinks it's important to demystify the process of looking into the future:

> *Envisioning the future is a natural ability—all men and women have at least some capacity. Some become players of the Stradivarius, so to speak, and others never get more than squeaks out of the fiddle. The degree of success is determined by the openness that you want to apply.*
>
> *You make mistakes when you start—it's a learning process, because you're learning a new way of thinking about things.*

McMoneagle sees a direct relationship between how we envision the future and how it will be. He believes that "we do, in fact, create our realities"—literally, through our intentions—and that "the only limitation on what the future might be occurs in our own minds . . . the birthplace of limitations."

If so—and even if not literally so—it behooves the person envisioning the future to project a positive one and not to block the view with unnecessary assumptions:

> *Expectations can actually get in the way. There seems to be a point where you can know too much about your problem. It's as if you leave yourself with only so many options. If you're envisioning the solution to a problem, there seems to be a point at which you want to let creativity take care of it. In other words, you don't want to get your feet stuck in some kind of rut, going in one direction.*

> *That step when you say, "What's it going to be like ten years from now?" should probably be done first, before you consider anything else, any details. Then nothing gets in the way; you haven't "prebuilt" the roads or directions that you will allow. Were you to try to cover all the bases first, all the things you know and assume in the present, and then try to envision the future, you'd be stuck with roads going north, south, east, and west—when it may be that there's no road at all and what gets you there is a path of a different nature.*

Use the Envision-the-Future approach, either on your own or in a meeting. I guarantee that you'll come up with ideas, many of which will be wacky, and a few of which could change your life.

Envision the Future

Visualize your problem as solved and then work back from the solution to the steps needed to achieve it.

Step 1 State your problem.

Step 2 What is your solution deadline?

Step 3 Visualize your ideal solution.

Project yourself mentally to a point in the future where the problem has been solved. Explore how it looks "out there" with the problem solved and finally describe how the problem was overcome.

Step 4 Stay in the future.

What are the news media saying about your performance? Write a headline and a brief newspaper story or thirty-second news brief.

Step 5 Record the phases leading up to your solution.

Staying "out there" in the future, "turn around" and "look back" toward today. What were the main stages or events that led to the problem's being solved?

Step 6 Overcome the barriers.

What were the major barriers overcome at each key stage in the solution process?

Step 7 Solution.

Now come back to the present and create a "first draft" of how you would solve the problem.

Chapter 7

YIN/YANG
Thinking in Opposites

Big: little. Up: down. The world is a world of opposites. Of course, any attribute, concept, or idea is meaningless without its opposite.

Thinkers and achievers have always been aware of the interplay of opposites. In the sixth century B.C., Lao-tzu wrote *Tao-te Ching*, which stressed the need for the successful leader to see opposites all around: "The wise leader knows how to be creative. In order to lead, the leader learns to follow. In order to prosper, the leader learns to live simply. In both cases, it is the interaction that is creative."

In the arts, opposites drive the creative process. The poet Samuel Taylor Coleridge observed that the power of the poet "reveals itself in the balance or reconciliation of opposite or discordant qualities." Thinking in opposites must have influenced Leonardo da Vinci when he painted his masterpiece—not simply because the enigmatic smile of *Mona Lisa* closely resembles an upside-down image of da Vinci's scowl in his own self-portrait, but in a larger sense because of the tension between the expected convention of a smile and the subject's unforgettable expression.

> **CREATIVE RULE OF THUMB #11**
>
> **All behavior consists of opposites. . . . Learn to see things backward, inside out, and upside down.**
> —Lao-tzu, *Tao-te Ching*

Closer to home, Richard Saul Wurman (*Information Anxiety*) says, "I love the space on my desk better than the objects themselves. It makes me see clearer. The opposites of things are just so much more fascinating than the things themselves. I look for a solution that has a valid oppositeness. Not a 'different' way of looking at things, but an opposite way. To see the opposite is illuminating." Charles Handy, in his book *The Age of Unreason* (Cambridge, Mass.: Harvard Business School Press, 1990), says that we're in a time of changes that are "discontinuous" or "without pattern"—an era that demands "upside-down, inside-out, and backward thinking."

To see the opposite, indeed, forms one of the primary techniques of idea making. Successful Idea Generators routinely look at problems in completely "opposed" ways. They look to see not only what a problem or idea *is* but what it *isn't*.

Opposites in the Marketplace

AT&T wanted to reach out and touch its preferred customers, those who held AT&T credit cards. In brainstorming various promotional schemes, they asked what can you do with a telephone and proceeded to come up with all sorts of ideas: you can make sales, make dates, buy something, find out about something, send computer messages, send fax messages, teleconference. . . . Big deal.

Then somebody had an inspiration. Don't ask what you can do with a telephone, ask what you *can't* do with it. So they began to brainstorm: you can't sleep with it, you can't put it in your pocket, you can't smoke it, you can't eat it, you can't drink it.

Eat it. You can't eat a telephone. Who says you can't? So AT&T sent out chocolate telephones as tokens of appreciation to its credit card holders.

A manufacturer of baby-bottle nipples faced a dilemma of corporate life-threatening proportions. Births were down. Breastfeeding was up. Sales were off. Either they found new consumers of baby-bottle nipples or they found new consumers of something else. Looking at the problem from the opposite perspective, they began to describe not only what a baby-bottle nipple was but what it *was not*. It was small, it was not large. It was used by babies and their parents who wanted those babies, it was not used by parents who did not want those babies. It had a hole in the end so the milk could get out, it was not totally solid to prevent the escape of liquids. *Not* large, not solid, not used by parents who did not want children. And thus did they solve their problem.

They started manufacturing condoms.

A company with twenty-eight thousand miles of unused oil pipeline wanted to move into new businesses. To come up with new sources of revenue, they thought backward—in opposites. Instead of pumping something through the pipeline, they could install something that would just sit there and not move at all: the networks of fiber-optic cable needed for the new long-distance phone companies. Companies like MCI Communications were only too happy to "pump" phone calls through the otherwise empty pipes.

A host of innovations come from the use of opposites. Some enterprising ad agencies broke away from regular print media advertising when they started looking at their medium—glossy magazines— from the opposite perspective. Print media ads placed a premium on sensations of sight, so agencies had traditionally concentrated on photography, copy, graphics, and overall design. After all, you could only touch the medium and see the medium. What could you *not* do with glossy paper? You couldn't smell it and you couldn't listen to it. That's no longer so: Check out the perfume ads and those that come with cut-out records.

> *Opposite thinking helped companies transform unused oil pipeline into optical cable networks—and baby-bottle nipple manufacturing into the making of condoms.*

Systematically Looking for Opposites

The Idea Generators of this world routinely look at things from different perspectives. One way they gain that different perspective is by looking at things backward. Though they may not know it, they use opposites in a rather systematic way. First, they tend to change positive statements into negative ones. Second, they try to define what something is *not*. Third, they try to figure out what everybody else doesn't. Fourth, they use what I call a "What If" Compass. Fifth, they change the direction or location of their perspective. Sixth, they flip-flop results. And seventh, they turn defeat into victory or victory into defeat. Let's visit each device in turn.

Make the Statement Negative

The first technique is the most obvious one but contains some nuances that you might not have thought about. All languages contain negative expressions enabling the speaker or writer to turn a positive expression into a negative one. Placing "no" or "not" before nouns, verbs, adjectives, and adverbs turns the positive into the negative.

Consider the problem faced by a manufacturer with a quality-control problem, a problem that inevitably irked and hassled its customers. Here's a positive statement—with a noun, a verb, an adjective, and an adverb—describing the problem:

All hassled customers complain loudly.

Now watch what happens when each element of the sentence is turned into a negative. Following each revised statement are the mental musings of an Idea Generator.

All hassled customers do not complain loudly.

Hmmmmm . . . If they do not complain, maybe they compliment us, maybe they thank us. How to get a hassled customer to thank us. Ahhh, call them and solve the quality problem immediately . . . maybe even before they know there's a problem.

Not all hassled customers complain loudly.

Whoops, there must be many hassled customers who just take their lumps, never complain, *and* never return. We've got to survey our customers and see if there are any we need to follow up with.

All hassled customers complain not loudly.

Uh oh. If they don't complain loudly, they complain softly. Not only here but elsewhere. There goes the word-of-mouth advertising so crucial to our success. We've got to identify our hassled customers and actively intervene so they are assured of our future quality and feel good about us as a supplier.

You can readily see how the device of making the statement negative alerted the Idea Generator to some very real problems in dire need of creative solutions. By making the verb negative, by thinking of "not complain," the Idea Generator thought of the opposite "to compliment, to thank." That train of thought led to the idea for an immediate response. By making the adjective "all" negative, by changing the statement to "not all," the Idea Generator identified an even more dangerous problem—the silent customers who never return. And by making the adverb "loudly" negative, the Idea Generator identified those customers who whispered their complaints to members of their organization, and worse, to competitors.

Using *no* and *not* isn't the only way to make statements negative. Don't forget the rather handy device of antonyms. If something is fat, think about it as thin. If it's old, imagine it new. If something is up there, look at it down here. If you use a word processor for writing, become accustomed to using its thesaurus feature, which can give you immediate access to antonyms.

Another linguistic way to use Opposite Thinking is to use the prefixes that form opposites: *un-*, *non-*, and *dis-* when added to the beginning of a word will yield an opposite meaning.

The Negative Definition

Great ideas often come from thinking about what something isn't. We look not at what a problem is but at what the problem is not. The English language itself encourages this approach to thinking with what is called the "correlative conjunction." Without getting too grammatical, one correlative conjunction is the "not . . . but" conjunction. As I stated above, we look "not" at what a problem is "but" at what a problem is not.

A colleague of mine publishes a job-search guide entitled *Does Your Resume Wear Blue Jeans?* In the very first chapter, the author used the negative definition approach to define a résumé. He defined what a résumé is by showing what it isn't: A résumé is not *Cover Girl* or *Esquire*, so, as a rule, no pictures. A résumé is not your Social Security card, so don't include your Social Security number. A résumé is not one of the Dead Sea Scrolls, so use modern top-quality paper. A résumé is not a birth certificate, so, as a rule, leave out your birthday. By thinking in terms of opposites, by defining what a résumé isn't, this author told the reader what a résumé is and made the topic of résumé writing come alive.

The Negative Definition device is, of course, quite simple. Just plug in the word or phrase you're trying to define and define what it is *not*:

> *[Word] or [Phrase] is not a . . .*

Proceed to jot down as many things the problem is not and you'll be surprised at the insights gained.

Here's an example. Suppose my problem is "poor quality control." Instead of looking at what poor quality control *is*, I look at what poor quality control *is not*.

Poor quality control is not . . .

> *profitable*
>
> *fun*
>
> *ethical*
>
> *efficient*

Now you continue with the exercise. Fill in five more things that poor quality control *is not:*

1. _____

2. _____

3. _____

4. _____

5. _____

By looking at what poor quality control is *not,* you gain a different perspective on what it *is* and how to go about achieving superior quality control.

Doing What Everybody Else Doesn't . . .

Anyone who is a parent has heard this lament: "But everybody else does it . . . ." Ah, peer pressure. In the marketplace, of course, it's called "competition," and certainly everyone playing in the marketplace keeps a close eye on what the competition does, what the consumer does, what the government does, and so on.

But you can flip-flop this perspective and think about "What everybody else doesn't do. . . ." This opposite perspective will help you identify those niches that no one else has discovered. You look not at what manufacturers are making, buyers are buying, teachers are teaching, regulators are regulating. Look instead to see what they are *not* making, buying, teaching, or regulating. By seeing what is *not* happening, you might just uncover what *ought to happen.*

One need not look far to find examples of the Everybody-Else-

Doesn't approach to idea making. First, Apple Computer saw what IBM was not doing. IBM was not making small computers for the little guy. Naturally, the little guys were not buying small computers because everybody else was not making them. Apple proceeded to do just that. Second, the Japanese saw quite clearly what Detroit was not doing. The Big Three were not producing small, fuel-efficient cars. The Japanese started doing just that and changed the way the world does business. Peter Lynch, author of *One Up on Wall Street* (New York: Penguin Books, 1989), uses this approach in seeing when the stock market will turn up. In his words: "When ten people at a cocktail party would rather talk to a dentist about plaque than to the manager of an equity mutual fund about stocks, it's likely that the market is about to turn up."

I've used the Everybody-Else-Doesn't approach many times in my business life. Once I was owed a considerable amount of money and discovered to my horror that my debtor was about to move out of town. I sat down and thought about what everybody else *does* do in order to get a handle on what everybody else *doesn't* do. Everybody else sends a formal invoice (I'll send a cartoon of myself lying on the floor with a giant knife stuck in my back and caption saying, "I trusted you."). Everybody else sends the invoice to the office where the secretary opens it (I'll send the cartoon to his home where he or his family will open it). Everybody else sends an invoice in a neatly typed business-size envelope (I'll send my cartoon in a three-foot package with a hand-addressed mailing label). Everybody else sends an invoice through the mail (I'll send mine by next-day UPS so that it'll be sitting on his doorstep when he gets home from the office).

My Everybody-Else-Doesn't approach to Opposite Thinking really paid off. Not only did I collect my bill, but I turned those collection cartoons into a novelty item, marketing them to stationery stores across the country. Stories appeared in many U.S. newspapers and then spread to Japan, Germany, and even Pakistan. I've been told that they were shown on the *Tonight Show*.

The "What If" Compass

The "What If" Compass is a device I use to facilitate thinking in opposites. I have a running list of pairs of opposing actions, which I've shared with you below. I add to the list all the time (and I encourage you to do the same). When I've got a problem, I just ask "What if I _____,"
and then I plug in each one of the opposite pairs of actions. By answering "what if" I invariably come up with some great ideas, all spawned by the Opposite Thinking approach to idea making.

Here's the list of opposing actions:

What if I . . .

Stretch it	*Shrink it*
Make it romantic	*Make it terrifying*
Combine it	*Separate it*
Appeal to kids	*Appeal to seniors*
Winterize it	*Summerize it*
Illuminate it	*Darken it*
Speed it up	*Slow it down*
Go clockwise	*Go counterclockwise*
Sharpen it	*Dull it*
Freeze it	*Melt it*
Misspell it	*Spell it correctly*
Sweeten it	*Sour it*
Balance it	*Unbalance it*
Tighten it	*Loosen it*
Force it	*Relax it*
Build it up	*Tear it down*
Tie it	*Untie it*
Jump over it	*Go under it*
Raise the price	*Give it away*

Put it to music	*Put it in pictures*
Add nostalgic appeal	*Add future appeal*
Make it stronger	*Make it weaker*
Make it portable	*Make it stationary*
Personalize it	*Depersonalize it*
Exaggerate it	*Understate it*
Put in sex appeal	*Take out sex appeal*
Make it simple	*Make it complex*
Fill it up	*Empty it*
Make it breakable	*Make it unbreakable*
Make it funny	*Make it serious*
Moisten it	*Dry it*
Cushion it	*Prick it*
Make it disposable	*Make it reusable*
Make it fly	*Make it float*
Do it backward	*Do it sideways*
Magnetize it	*Demagnetize it*
Make it invisible	*Make it visible*
Go forward	*Go backward*

Changing Directions or Locations

The Change Direction or Location approach to idea making requires you to do one of two things: Either you physically change your perspective by getting off your, uh, chair and going somewhere else, or you mentally change the way something works or the direction something takes or the vantage point from which you watch something work.

Certainly the "Managing By Wandering Around" (MBWA) technique made famous by Hewlett-Packard uses the device of physically changing one's perspective. The manager actually gets off his or her seat, goes among the people he or she directs, watches what goes on, talks to people about their problems, and then comes up with some great ideas.

Mentally changing perspectives requires a highly developed imagination. If you look at something from the top down, look at it from the bottom up. If you're on the outside, mentally go inside and check things out. If something goes left to right, make it go right to left.

IBM used this Change Direction approach when it revolutionized typewriters. Remember the old Underwoods (and Remingtons, and IBMs, etc.) with the black-and-red cloth ribbons? The entire carriage holding the paper moved from right to left as the stationary keys typed the line from left to right. IBM changed all that by reversing the directions. It figured out how to keep the paper still and move the typing element. The paper stayed put, the typing ball moved from left to right. Typewriting would never be the same again.

Flip-Flop Results

If your desired result is "Better Morale," flip-flop this result and think about producing the opposite—really rotten morale. What would it take to make everyone go screaming from the room, refusing to work at such an awful place? By turning around the results, you begin to look at the problem from the completely opposite perspective.

This approach, of course, is nothing new. Ever heard of the Devil's advocate? If you want to increase sales, think about decreasing them. What would you have to do to produce truly awful sales results? Flip-flopping the results will give you a completely opposite perspective on the problem. Changing the perspective often produces some great ideas.

Recently the New England office of the U.S. Environmental Protection Agency executed a brilliant example of flip-flopping results, as well as doing what everyone else doesn't. They developed a public awareness campaign called "How to Destroy the Earth." Its tips included:

Leave lights on

Photocopy everything

Buy overpackaged products

Ask for plastic supermarket bags

Drive everywhere (don't walk, bicycle, or take public transportation)

Reach for paper towels (why use one made of cloth?)

Pour used motor oil into the ground

Mow your lawn daily

Throw leaves out with the trash

Put off that tune-up ("if only one hundred thousand car owners followed this simple tip, we'd add ninety million pounds of greenhouse gases to the air")

The campaign drove its message home with this opposite punchline: "You can save the earth by knowing what you are doing to destroy it."

Snatching Victory from the Jaws of Defeat

The Idea Generator will often snatch victory from the jaws of defeat. When you're staring defeat in the face, just declare yourself a winner and see what happens.

A publisher friend of mine recently used this device to turn a bad situation into increased book sales. Another publishing company had mistakenly printed my friend's toll-free telephone number on more than fifty thousand promotional pieces mailed nationwide. The phones lighted up, with useless calls that disrupted staff time and cost quite a bit of money in 800-toll charges. Figuring that it had to pay a one-minute minimum toll anyway, the president of the company alerted the staff to get the caller's name and address and to send a catalog of the company's books. Now instead of cursing the unwanted phone calls, the company profits from them.

Attractive Opposites

Casting your problem in opposite terms is one of the most potent ways to dream up great ideas. To help you reap the benefits of Opposite Thinking, I've prepared the Great Idea Action Sheets that follow.

The Power of Opposite Thinking

After stating a problem, come up with some great ideas by (1) making the statement negative, (2) coming up with a negative definition, and (3) figuring out what everybody else doesn't do.

Problem statement:

Step 1 Make the statement negative. Make various parts of the statement negative by adding *no, not, non-, un-, dis-,* or an antonym to the statement.

Step 2 Negative definition. First define what the problem is and then define what it is *not*.

Step 3 What everybody else doesn't. Write down what everybody else is doing (competitors, customers, government, private sector, and other relevant players). Then write down what they are *not* doing.

DOING	NOT DOING
_____	_____
_____	_____
_____	_____

Step 4 Pick a possible solution.

_____

_____

_____

The "What If" Compass

Briefly describe your problem. Then pick two opposing actions such as "increase it/decrease it" from the list of opposing actions given earlier in this chapter. Complete the "What If" question as many times as you can and show the various results. Jot down resulting ideas.

Problem statement:

Step 1 Ask yourself, What if I . . . _____
Results

1. _____

2. _____

3. _____

4. _____

Step 2 Ask yourself, What if I . . . _____
Results

1. _____

2. _____

3. _____

4. _____

Step 3 Write down ideas that will help solve the problem.

_____

_____

_____

_____

What a Great Idea! Copyright © 1992 by Charles "Chic" Thompson.

Changing Perspectives

Briefly describe your problem. In the space provided, come up with some great ideas by (1) changing the direction of the process or your location in viewing the problem, (2) changing the results to exactly the opposite, and (3) transforming the problem into an opportunity.

Problem statement:

Step 1 **Change directions or locations.** Write down changes in the direction of the process or in your vantage point in viewing the problem.

Step 2 **Flip-flop results.** State the exact opposite of the results you are experiencing. Note how you could produce these opposite results.

Step 3 **Snatching victory from the jaws of defeat.** Take the problem and turn it into an opportunity. How can you profit from the problem?

Step 4 **Record your new ideas.** After studying your notes, write down three ideas that will help solve the problem.

Chapter 8

FREE DESSERT
Challenging Assumptions

Because I travel a great deal, I eat most of my meals at restaurants. The result is that I've gotten wrong entrées quite a few times. On one of these occasions, I got an additional surprise. I told the waiter about the problem; he gave the expected response and apologized. But when he brought my new entrée, the waiter also brought back the menu—and asked me to select a free dessert. I found myself thanking him.

I thanked the waiter for his mistake!

It then dawned on me what the restaurant had done. I sought out the manager and asked him how they had come up with the idea of offering free desserts.

"Simple," he said. "We had a meeting about mistakes that give customers a hassle, to find some ways to reduce that hassle. We all agreed we should apologize.

"Someone then said, 'Why not get the customer to thank us?' I asked how. 'Well,' he said, 'if our mistakes hassle the customers, let's make it up to them and give them something for it. That way, they'll end up thanking us.'"

"It's unbelievable," the manager said, "but now our customers do thank us when we make mistakes. And our performance has actually improved because we're thinking more about customer service, not worrying about screwing up an order."

This restaurant used a terrific device for generating great ideas: it challenged ingrained assumptions. The assumption: that there was nothing the restaurant could do to undo its mistake or the customer's anger. The situation was simply a hassle for the customer, and no apology could take that hassle away. The customer

> **CREATIVE RULE OF THUMB #12**
>
> **Challenging an assumption can turn obstacles into opportunities.**

would complain—period. Challenging the assumption erased the self-fulfilling prophecy.

As I mentioned in Chapter 2, top executives at Steelcase, Inc., wanted a design for their corporate development center that would foster creative solutions to the problems of competing in the twenty-first century. When commissioning their design from the architects, they challenged the assumption that a center is divided into departments. The resulting plans produced an environment that requires finance to mingle with sales, with product design, with advertising. The "clustered teams" design brings together four members, one from each department. The pyramid building structure gives everyone a window, and features a large, quiet room at the apex—a room for reflection, research, and private brainstorming.

According to Steelcase, the center is now a laboratory of innovation. They named the new design "functional inconvenience."

Recently, I was asked to adapt a successful training program for the General Electric salaried work force to the hourly factory work force. Many underlying assumptions surfaced rapidly:

> *The director of operations summed up the results of challenging assumptions when he spoke to the hourly workers. "You blew them away," he said, "with your great presentations."*

1. The factory work force could never sit through a two-day course, so reduce it to one.

2. The factory work force could never make presentations to management; they just don't have the presentation skills. So eliminate that part of the training.

3. The factory work force will never speak out if their supervisors and team leaders are in the room, so only include employees from the first three pay levels.

Naturally, we challenged many of these assumptions. And we produced one of the most empowering training programs of my career. It featured a cross-functional and multilayered mix of factory employees interacting and presenting for *two consecutive days*. We invited supervisors and team leaders to help with presentations, and you couldn't tell the "ties" from the "hourlies" because everyone in attendance was required to wear a GE T-shirt—even the executive vice president of manufacturing.

We instructed the factory workers in the use of various visual aids for their presentations. Many of their presentations turned out to be more to the point and more emotional than those produced by the salaried personnel.

The closing comments of the director of operations to the factory employees summed up the powerful effects of challenging these ingrained assumptions: "You blew management away with your great presentations. We've known that you have the answers to help us. We just didn't know how to listen for them. I'm so proud of you." As he turned to walk back to his seat, I noticed tears in his eyes. And in everyone else's. A wall had come crashing down.

Challenging assumptions, as you can plainly see, is quite simple. To come up with ideas, you must reframe your problem or situation. Challenge the normal assumptions one makes when dealing with such problems or when defining such goals.

1. *Define your problem.*

2. *Write down all assumptions that you would ordinarily make in the many facets of that problem.*

3. *Challenge each assumption by making it a negative or an opposite. If you assume that centers are broken into departments, assume the negative that they're not and analyze what might happen if the assumption is false. If you assume that hassled customers only complain, assume the opposite that they express gratitude; you may then be able to imagine how this would be possible.*

Un-creation, *Re*-creation

Looking at the world creatively is really a matter of *re*-creation, which implies a certain amount of *un*creation—undoing, if only in your imagination, things that "everybody knows are so." If our assumptions were all true, we would never be surprised, and nothing new would ever be created. Every assumption we have is an opportunity for change, fun, improvement—an opening for your great idea.

Challenging Assumptions

Write down your assumptions relating to the problem stated below. Then challenge each of these assumptions and jot down ideas coming from each challenge.

Problem statement:

Step 1 Write down three assumptions that we ordinarily make when confronted with this problem.

1. _____

2. _____

3. _____

Step 2 Now challenge each assumption by stating its opposite or by assuming the negative.

1. _____

2. _____

3. _____

Step 3 Write down potential advantages that could come from your challenges to these assumptions.

1. _____

2. _____

3. _____

Step 4 After studying the challenged assumptions, write down on another sheet of paper any suggestions you could use to solve the problem.

What a Great Idea! Copyright © 1992 by Charles "Chic" Thompson.

Chapter 9

NEW SHOES
Changing Perspectives

Take off your shoes. Put on somebody else's. Put on your customer's shoes. Put on your boss's. Try your husband's or wife's shoes on for size. See what the other person sees. Feel what the other person feels. Change your perspective, and you'll also change your ideas and come up with some great ones.

Picking Stocks

Peter Lynch, the famed and now former manager of the Magellan Mutual Fund, often changed his shoes to gain a unique perspective on the stock market. In his book *One Up on Wall Street*, he had this to say: "The stocks I try to buy are the very stocks that traditional fund managers try to overlook. In other words, I continue to think like an amateur as frequently as possible."

> **CREATIVE RULE OF THUMB #13**
>
> **If different shoes don't work, try looking at your problem from a helicopter . . . or a space ship.**

One could say that George Gribbins, former guiding force at Young & Rubicam ad agency, took *changing perspectives* to inhuman lengths. He would open the agency's "creative workshops" by lighting a candle and saying: "Imagine that you have died and have been reborn. You can come back to earth as anything you want to be *except* a human being. Now write down what you would like to be and why" (Norins, *The Young & Rubicam Traveling Creative Workshop*).

Stacking Chairs

Recently I was asked to serve on the advisory board of Architecture and Children, the mission of which is to design the school of the future. The board consists of architects, educators, school superintendents, computer manufacturers, and others interested in improving the quality of public education. In my work with the board, I had the pleasure of meeting Anne P. Taylor, author of *School Zone* (Corrales, N. Mex.: School Zone, Inc., 1983). To come up with ideas for unique and effective learning environments (ranging from seating arrangements to posters on the wall), Anne's researchers tried on the perspectives of children. In one experiment studying the importance of seating arrangements, the researchers removed all the desks in a classroom and had some stacking chairs waiting outside the classroom for the students to arrive. When they got to school, the teacher gave each child a chair outside the classroom and told the children to put the chairs wherever they wished. The "clusters" chosen by the children seemed to reduce hyperactivity and increase attention spans. The resulting designs certainly opened the eyes of the researchers and gave them vital perspectives they otherwise would not have.

Leading Others

In studying the qualities of good leaders, we have found that they routinely put on the shoes of people two levels above and below them. For example, midlevel executives should look at a problem from the perspective of their boss's boss and their direct staff's employees. This broad perspective, gained through the Change-Your-Shoes approach to creativity, enables the executive to function and communicate as a leader, not just as a manager. It encourages the creation of ideas that respond to the organization and its world as a system—and helps prevent ideas that only fix "my problem."

I look at leadership as a necessary quality for all managers who want to inspire their staff with creativity and to lead the process of innovation. To distill the essence of an essay by John P. Kotter ("What Leaders Really Do," *Harvard Business Review*, May–June 1990), the following qualities of leadership and good management are complementary:

Leadership	**Good Management**
Coping with change	*Bringing order and consistency*
Developing a vision	*Planning and budgeting*
Aligning people to the vision	*Organizing and staffing*
Motivating and inspiring	*Controlling and monitoring*

Changing Shoes

Using the Change-Your-Shoes approach is easy.

1. *Take off your shoes.*

2. *Identify as many people as possible who are in some way connected with the problem you're trying to solve.*

3. *Put on their shoes.*

4. *Imagine what the problem looks like to them.*

5. *Jot down ideas that come from your changed perspective.*

By the way, I have it on good authority that the CEO of HarperCollins, publisher of this book, takes the shoe-changing idea quite literally. Before he leads brainstorming sessions, he changes from his work shoes into a pair of slippers—an excellent way to encourage a more flexible frame of mind.

Change Your Shoes

Assume the viewpoints of others to help find solutions to your problem.

Problem statement:

Step 1 Write down the identities of three people who ordinarily are associated with the problem.

1. _____

2. _____

3. _____

Step 2 Now describe the problem from their points of view.

1. _____

_____

2. _____

_____

3. _____

_____

Step 3 After studying the identities of these three people and their differing perspectives, write down suggestions we could use to solve the problem.

_____

_____

_____

_____

Chapter 10

A CURVE BALL
Metaphorical Thinking

Highly creative people often use comparisons—similes and metaphors—to help define problems and to think about possible solutions. They look at their problem, define it, and perhaps even give it a name. They then think metaphorically, ruminating about what their problem is like. To create a simile, for example, one need only say:

"My problem is like a _____."

I use *metaphor* here in a broad sense, to refer to similes, metaphors, and other figures of speech that create comparisons between things. Thinking metaphorically serves several important functions:

1. *Metaphors enable you to go beyond the limits of standard solutions through divergent thinking and to move away from the problem so you can see the bigger picture.*

2. *Metaphors focus your mind on relationships of ideas, images, and symbols.*

3. *Metaphors make complex issues easier to understand.*

4. *Metaphors create tension—collisions of ideas—and fusion— an integration of ideas.*

5. *Metaphors turn one idea into two or more.*

Blasts from the Past

We've always used metaphors to describe our problems and guide decisions in the workplace. The resulting metaphors have infused our language with colorful and incisive images.

At the start of the industrialized period, we used the machine metaphor and spoke essentially of survival. Our goal was to keep business going, to keep the machine "well oiled." When faced with problems, we "hammered out the details."

As war consumed much of the twentieth century, military metaphors hit the workplace: "Let's win the battle in the trenches!" "Let's go at them with both barrels!" The notion of hostile competition had been added to our formula for success.

By the 1950s, competition in warfare was replaced with a more civil form of competition—the athletic arena. Our organizations mirrored the structure of athletic teams and our motivational cry was for team spirit. Strategic language sounded like it came from a locker room. A common warning was: "Watch out! They might throw us a curve!" While on the playing field, we found the competition still hostile, for someone had to lose.

In the Groove

As we move through the information age, successful organizations will make the transition to the next step in metaphors. Organizations are beginning to "march to a different beat." Now we're "improvising." *Improvisation* is at the heart of today's favorite type of metaphor—the music metaphor.

Management guru Peter Drucker, using the music metaphor, compares the successful information-based corporation to a symphony orchestra. This metaphor requires highly talented specialists to perform at their peak to play great music.

CREATIVE RULE OF THUMB #14

Think like Nature. Ask "How would Nature solve this problem?"
—Jonas Salk[1]

A Walk in the Woods

The next metaphorical frontier most likely lies in nature. As ecological political movements begin to appeal to the middle class, as the media continue to explore the hazards facing Mother Earth, and as we realize that beneficial

1. *A World of Ideas with Bill Moyers*, "The Science of Hope with Jonas Salk," PBS Video.

change comes from evolution not revolution, I believe that the next operative metaphor will emphasize "nature's way of doing things." For unlike our former metaphors of war and athletic prowess and their emphasis on winning and losing, nature provides an appropriate win/win metaphor, allowing us more room for incorporating our creative feelings and for instilling a long-term sense of global cooperation.

Win/Lose vs. Win/Win Metaphors

Both types of metaphors have their place in history and in fulfilling our present managerial needs. Skilled communicators and Idea Generators mix and pace their use of these two types of metaphor to gain immediate motivation and foster long-term cooperation with their vision. The win/lose (military and sports) and win/win (nature and music) metaphors likely inspire different reactions within an organization:

Win/Lose (Military & Sports)	Win/Win (Nature & Music)
Immediate motivation	*Incremental motivation*
Revolution	*Evolution*
Competition	*Cooperation*
Inspiration	*Contemplation*
Production oriented	*Information oriented*
Mission statements	*Vision statements*

Playing with the Sports Metaphor

When your goal is team building, the sports metaphor offers valuable insight. To have a winning team, you need to ask these questions:

1. Is our team playing the right game?

2. Does our team have the right players?

3. Is the coach's leadership style right for our team?

By definition, a team is two or more persons with a shared goal that cannot be accomplished effectively by one person acting alone. To help expand your use of the sports metaphor, I've organized a comparison of three popular sports on the next page.

Perhaps an even better metaphor than basketball for the collaborative type of organizational effort is rugby. A case study of Honda, cited in Michael Schrage's *Shared Minds*, quotes a Honda manager:

> *I am always telling the [new-product development] team members that our work is not a relay race—that's my work and yours starts here. Every one of us should run all the way from the start to the finish. Like in a rugby game, all of us should run together, passing the ball left and right and reaching the goal as one united body.*

Mastering the Music Metaphor

Managers and musicians, CEOs and conductors are surprisingly similar. An orchestral score is much like the five-year plan, which guides both large and small organizations. The musical notes guide the conductor and instrumentalists just as organizational guidelines direct executives, managers, and staff.

All musical ensembles, from small jazz combos to rock bands to large symphony orchestras, involve organization and cooperation. Each group typically has a leader, the conductor in a large orchestra leading the group in its musical interpretation and coordinating the members during performance, the small jazz combo often relying on a soloist to coordinate the overall effect and sound.

The music metaphor applies especially to organizations, for much of today's music incorporates flexibility and innovation. Jazz thrives on creative tension. According to Miles Davis, musical innovation arose from a friction between his technique and the band members' evolving sense of community and purpose. In his words:

> *I don't lead musicians, man. They lead me. I listen to them and learn what they do best.*

Jazz musicians constantly seek a new sound, a new combination, a new feel, a new expression. If we accept change as a premise for the future of our world, then that same desire to explore new sounds, feels, or combinations is the asset organizations need to keep pace with the marketplace of goods, services, and political ideas.

Sports Metaphor Matrix for Business

Styles of:	Football	Baseball	Basketball
Coaching	Call right plays	Choose right players	Develop self-correcting team
Communication	Top down	Up and down	Up, down, and among
Leadership	Authoritarian	Laissez-faire	Facilitative
Team	Loyalty	Autonomy	Interdependence
Success	Consistent execution	Big individual plays	Continuous adaptation
Player	Waits for decision	Self-directed	Proactive, interdependent
Type of:			
Organization	Manufacturing Fast-food industry	Sales organizations Technical units	Hi-tech firms Project teams
Environment	Consistent, structured Centrally controlled	Changing, unstructured Individual concentration	Rapidly changing Group creativity

Talking in Music

The music metaphor permeates our language with an array of sayings that evoke many moods and meanings. Have you ever caught yourself asking how a given plan will be "orchestrated" or what "mode" it's in? The following phrases have already worked themselves into our standard office vocabulary:

You're marching to a different drum.

We've got a lot of dissonance here.

We're playing in harmony.

Our section is out of tune.

Let's improvise.

Let's try it in a different key.

Using Music Metaphors

You can use music metaphors in any situation simply by thinking of your problem in musical terms. This metaphor is best suited for situations that require harmonizing of conflicts or different points of view. Try completing the Great Idea Action Sheet on page 124 to see how music metaphors might harmonize your office environment.

The Nature Metaphor

Great thinkers often turn to nature for inspiration. By comparing a problem to a similar occurrence in nature, otherwise elusive great ideas often introduce themselves to your mind. Dr. Louis Pasteur, for example, noticed that the skin of grapes had to be broken before the fermentation process of winemaking could begin. Pasteur then realized that man's skin had to be broken before infection occurred—a great leap from that day's theory that infection was caused by internal poisonous gases.

Thomas Edison used the nature metaphor to invent whole systems such as a lamp, a conduit, and a dynamo. In his words: "Nature doesn't just make leaves; it makes branches and trees and roots to go with them." Charles Darwin used branches to illustrate his "tree of life," which led to his theory of evolution. And of course, Sir Isaac Newton, while "in a contemplative mood," was inspired by "the fall of an apple" to develop the laws of gravity.

Looking at your problem or goal through the eyes of nature is an especially useful technique when you need to expand your horizons. Try it out in the Great Idea Action Sheet on page 125.

Metaphors in Action

In consulting with public and private organizations, I have often used or encountered the metaphor-making approach to innovation and idea generation.

Federal Government

I was working with a federal agency that had just installed hundreds of new PC computers, which were replacing older microcomputers. A lot of the older, senior managers weren't very friendly with either the old computer system or the new PCs. They used to have older computers on their desks. They didn't use them. Now they had new PCs on their desks. They didn't use them either. The agency had also paid for self-instructional computer training programs. But still the older managers balked. The agency opened a learning resource center, which had PCs and interactive videodisks for self-instruction. The young people in the agency would flock to the resource center and eagerly engage in instructional programs to learn the new computer system. Indeed, the younger employees had taken over the resource center and arranged for rock music to be piped in. The older employees refused to go in and learn the system.

The agency mentioned the problem to me during a workshop I was conducting. To solve the problem, I tried to think of a metaphor that describes why these older managers weren't using the new computer system.

Watching the managers walk through the resource center reminded me of the first time I went into an Oriental rug store. To be in step with my neighbors, I knew I needed some Oriental rugs for my new condo. So I found a renowned Oriental rug store, parked my car, and walked in. There before me on the floor of this showroom were expensive Oriental rugs all over the floor. I gingerly walked in, careful not to step on the rugs, choked, and walked out.

A few days later, I was visiting a new neighbor. He had several Oriental rugs, and lo and behold, people actually walked on them. I realized that Oriental rugs indeed were made for walking, lounging, resting, loving. I returned to the Oriental rug store, this time confidently striding on expensive Oriental rugs. I even asked for and received a "loaner" to take home to try on for size.

> The city managers found it helpful to compare their proposed parking garage to a refrigerator.

Back at the government agency, I asked, "Aren't the senior executives wondering whether they can touch these computers? If they push the wrong button, aren't they afraid of crashing the program?" (Aren't they wondering whether they can step on Oriental rugs?)

Thinking about computers and the resource center in this way sparked some creative solutions. The agency decided to provide take-home laptop PCs with audiocassette or VCR self-instruction. (A take-home Oriental rug loaner.) Senior management was shown that they could indeed step on an Oriental rug, that a computer indeed could help solve problems they faced in their day-to-day jobs.

Local Government

Kalamazoo, Michigan, used a metaphor to sell its ideas to the city council. The city management had to show the need for a parking garage to city council. I brainstormed with the city management team and asked them to create a metaphor to show the need for a parking garage and to show how it would blend in with the surrounding community. After a host of suggestions, one of the group's members suggested that a parking garage was like a refrigerator. Just as a garage temporarily holds a car, a refrigerator temporarily holds food. The item going in had to be preserved. Its value coming out had to be the same as its value going in. The refrigerator must blend in with the kitchen in color, shape, design, and cost.

The planning team then created a presentation to the city council likening the garage to a refrigerator. The city council was receptive because the metaphor simplified the presentation. It immediately understood the need for the garage and especially the need for it to blend in with the surroundings of the community.

Private Enterprise

Jack Welch, CEO of General Electric, declared war on junk work and, in eliminating it, decided to make speed, simplicity, and self-confidence GE's standard way of running its worldwide businesses.

Welch used a most effective metaphor to describe the need for speed, simplicity, and self-confidence. He asked a group of top managers how many had moved their residences within the past ten years. Most raised their hands. He then asked how many had moved half-full cans of paint and pairs of stained sneakers used to stain wooden decks. Most raised their hands. He then asked how many had *used* those cans of paint and sneakers *ever* in their new homes. Only a few hands appeared.

Welch then pointed out that the same thing happens when people change positions. They take previously necessary reports, approvals, meetings, measurements, and policies with them to their new jobs. It was these, Welch believed, that slowed people down. What was needed instead was a healthy "spring cleaning."

This spring cleaning, called "Work-Out!," now constitutes a ten-year plan at General Electric. To speed up people's performance, GE insists on a new mind-set of continuous improvement by finding a better way every day.

By focusing people's minds on the metaphor of half-full paint cans, stained sneakers, and spring cleaning, the General Electric CEO has managed to create an environment of speed and self-renewing innovation.

As you can see, creating metaphors can be quite effective as an approach to idea making. The process is simple.

1. Describe your problem.
   Senior management isn't using the new computers.
   We've got to sell a parking garage to city council.
   Our work performance needs speeding up.
2. Isolate the problem down to a single word or phrase:
   Computers
   Parking garage
   Unnecessary work
3. Dream up some metaphorical ideas by completing this simile:
   [Word] is like a . . .
   Computers are like Oriental rugs. People are afraid of them.
   A parking garage is like a refrigerator. It stores things.

> *Slow junk work is like half-full cans of paint. You keep moving them around with you and you don't ever use them.*

4. Use the metaphorical image and try to solve the metaphorical problem.
5. Be ready. All sorts of ideas will emerge from the process.

Juggling: A Metaphor for Workaday Life

Juggling, like your life at work and even at play, requires a balance between keeping a sharp focus on essentials and letting go of the unnecessary. Successful jugglers (and people in business, government, the professions) must focus on the pinnacle of their toss (their goals, their vision) and trust that their hands (their people, customers, clients) can throw and catch at the same time. Jugglers (and people in business, government, the professions) who are preoccupied with looking at their hands are actually looking for potential failures. They drop the ball. The same preoccupation can prevent you from communicating and achieving your vision. You drop the ball.

> *Jugglers, just like people in business and elsewhere, have to focus on the pinnacle of their toss—their vision—and trust their hands to throw and catch at the same time.*

In order to get GE employees to feel what it's like to focus on a shared vision while doing their daily tasks, I teach them the art of juggling. I emphasize that the juggler must focus attention on that pinnacle area, which I liken to a shared vision. If jugglers stop looking at the shared vision and lower their eyes to their hands, they will start dropping things.

Juggling is also simply a good way to loosen up a situation, and yourself. John Ahlbach, of the National Stuttering Project, recommends juggling as a way for speech pathologists to work with kids in schools—to create rapport, improve the juggler's self-image, teach a new behavior, make therapy more fun, and break "a few hand-held objects in your office you didn't want anyway."

And, he says, "Juggling makes that ordinary trip to the produce market a real adventure" (John Ahlbach, "Juggling and What It Can Do for You" [San Francisco: National Stuttering Project, n.d.]).

So get out three tennis balls or bean bags and get ready to become a juggler. (For more thorough instructions, see John Cassidy and B. C.

Rimbeaux, *Juggling for the Complete Klutz* [Stanford, Calif.: Klutz Press, 1977].)

How to Become a Juggler

Step One

Start with one ball in your throwing hand.

Step Two

Throw it from hand to hand with scooping underhand throws. Say "Throw" when you toss it, to distract yourself from worrying about catching it; trust yourself to catch and focus instead on throwing. The pinnacle should be slightly above your head. The pattern will form a figure eight. Keep your eyes focused at the top of your toss and your hands down at waist level.

Step Three

Now face a wall and put a ball in each hand. The wall forms a plane for your tossing pattern. Start tossing from your dominant throwing hand and say "One." When that ball reaches its peak, say "Two" and throw the second ball with your other hand. The two balls will cross in the air and change hands.

Step Four

You are probably throwing the second ball to the side or out in front of you. Keep going. It just takes some more practice to get your toss under control.

Step Five

Now start with two balls in your dominant throwing hand and a third in your other hand. Start tossing with your dominant hand and say "One." Say "Two" when the ball reaches its peak and toss the second ball, held in your nondominant hand. When that ball reaches its peak, say "Three" and toss the third ball, held in your dominant hand. When that ball reaches its peak, say "Four" and keep going.

Step Six

If you are having difficulty releasing the third ball, make a pact with yourself that no matter what, you will throw that ball. Don't try to make perfect tosses or to catch every ball.

Dropping the ball is a metaphor for progress.

What Game Are You Playing?

Compare the style of your organization with the three team sports illustrated in this chapter (football, baseball, basketball)—or with any sport familiar to you—or expand the metaphor to create a hybrid sport that best describes your organization.

Step 1 Fill out the sports metaphor chart below.

Your Styles of: Similar Sport:

Coaching _____   _____

_____

Communication _____   _____

_____

Leadership _____   _____

_____

Team _____   _____

_____

Success _____   _____

_____

Player _____   _____

_____

Your Type of:

Organization _____   _____

_____

Environment _____   _____

_____

Step 2 Now answer these questions:

1. What are your strengths as a team?

2. What are your weaknesses as a team?

3. What would a half-time locker room talk sound like?

4. Do you have superstars? Bench-warmers?

5. Is your coaching style right for the game?

6. How do you celebrate when you win?

7. How do you console and motivate when you lose?

Step 3 Review your answers and on another sheet of paper make your game plan for winning.

Using the Music Metaphor

Use a music metaphor Idea Map to come up with suggestions for managing stress in the office.

Step 1 Complete the following analogy:

Stress is like what in music: _____

Step 2 Idea Map your music metaphor on another sheet of paper.

Put your music metaphor in a circle in the center of your paper and start Idea Mapping. Write down as quickly as you can words associated with your music metaphor; put these words all around the center circle. Look for new associations. Draw arrows from one word to another connecting your key thoughts; add more words as necessary.

Step 3 Look for the main concepts and patterns in your Idea Map.

Assign geometric symbols to your main concepts and "cluster" your words by putting the respective symbol around each related word.

Step 4 Create an Idea Outline.

Now transcribe your Idea Map into either a "cluster" or a Roman-numeral outline.

Step 5 Record your ideas. Write down four ideas that can help you manage stress in your office.

Using the Nature Metaphor

Use a nature metaphor Idea Map to come up with suggestions for improving communications in the office.

Step 1 Complete the following analogy:

Effective communication is like what in nature: _____

Step 2 Idea Map your nature metaphor on another sheet of paper.

Put your nature metaphor in a circle in the center of your paper and start Idea Mapping. Write down as quickly as you can words associated with your nature metaphor; put these words all around the center circle. Look for new associations. Draw arrows from one word to another connecting your key thoughts; add more words as necessary.

Step 3 Look for the main concepts and patterns in your Idea Map.

Assign geometric symbols to your main concepts and "cluster" your words by putting the respective symbol around each related word.

Step 4 Create an Idea Outline.

Now transcribe your Idea Map into either a "cluster" or a Roman-numeral outline.

Step 5 Record your ideas. Write down four ideas that can help you improve communications in your office.

Create a Metaphor

Write down metaphors that describe or characterize the problem stated below.
From the metaphors, suggest positive ways to help solve the problem.

Problem statement:

Step 1 Reduce the problem to a word or short phrase:

WORD:

PHRASE:

Step 2 Insert your word or phrase to produce appropriate analogies:

[WORD] is like a:

[PHRASE] is like a:

Step 3 Pick the best, cleverest, most apt, or most unusual image from your analogies and proceed to try to solve your problem metaphorically.

Step 4 From the metaphorical solutions, write down two ideas that can help you solve your problem.

Chapter 11

THE BRAIN PICKERS
Borrowing from Others

I've got to be careful here, for there is Okay Borrowing and Not Okay Borrowing.

Okay Borrowing is simply borrowing an idea from someone else and improving on it. Okay Borrowing has been going on in the world of commerce for thousands of years and, if we're to progress, must go on indefinitely into the future.

Among the innumerable fields that reflect the benefits of Okay Borrowing is small appliances. In the 1920s, Hamilton Beach borrowed the idea behind the vacuum cleaner, combined it with their small food blender motor and . . . voilà! the portable hair dryer. Waring then borrowed the idea behind the malted drink blender from Hamilton Beach and introduced it into bars for mixed drinks. In the late 1950s, Oster borrowed the blender idea and introduced "Spin Cookery."

> **CREATIVE RULE OF THUMB #15**
>
> **Swipe from the best, then adapt.**
> —Tom Peters[1]

Not Okay Borrowing has also been going on since the dawn of time. It's called plagiarism, trademark infringement, patent infringement, or copyright infringement. In a word, stealing.

The difference between Okay Borrowing and Not Okay Borrowing, of course, is crucial. It might very well mean the difference between unbounded market success (Okay Borrowing) and a term in jail (Not Okay). Basically, it's Okay to take somebody else's idea and use it. For example, if McDonald's shows that there's a market in fast-food hamburgers, then it's perfectly Okay, indeed beneficial to the marketplace, for Hardee's and Wendy's to start up fast-food hamburger franchises.

---

1. Paraphrased from Peters, *Thriving on Chaos*.

The fast-food hamburger idea itself is too broad for anyone to own, as is the idea of franchises. But the expressions, formulations, and emblems particular to McDonald's implementation of the idea—for example, the Golden Arches—can be protected by a trademark at the U.S. Office of Patents & Trademarks. Advertising copy, packaging, and the like can also be protected by copyright. Using golden arches to sell hamburgers is a Not Okay form of Idea Borrowing.

The wise Idea Generator, indeed wise organizations, will make it a habit to become exposed to the ideas of others, to identify good ideas, and to adapt them for one's own beneficial purposes.

The Great Idea Network

Until recently, all employees at Nissan Motors were required to drive Nissan cars. That made sense, according to top management. It would certainly hurt the image of the company to have its employees preferring the cars of competitors.

No longer. Now Nissan's top management allows employees to own anyone's cars, and encourages employees to test-drive the cars of competitors, to visit competitors' showrooms, to look carefully at the ideas developed by others. They've stopped the mind-set that if it's "not invented here," it can't possibly be any good.

Dorothy Brunson, pioneering owner of Brunson Communications, a chain of radio and television stations in Baltimore, Atlanta, and Wilmington, North Carolina, has long used a like approach. As pointed out in Helgesen's *The Female Advantage,* Brunson, who created the influential black community-based call-in format for AM radio, keeps a close eye on the competition: "I have a policy. Everyone who works here has to spend two days a week listening to other stations, then report to me on what's going on. A lot of big radio networks have sophisticated monitoring equipment. *I* do everything by listening and by gut."

Many successful innovators recognize the value of borrowing ideas. They resist what others have called the "Not-Invented-Here" (NIH) syndrome. Even though I didn't coin this term, it's so apropos that I just can't resist borrowing it for my book. (Okay Borrowing.)

Creatively Borrowing Creativity

People get so hung up on the NIH syndrome that they close their eyes to ideas developed elsewhere. Most likely, arrogance explains the syndrome. Other likely causes include the Protestant ethic (if it's free, it can't be good; if it didn't require Herculean effort, it can't be worthwhile) or a sense of false pride (what *we* do is important, what *they* do can't possibly measure up to *our* standards). Whatever the source, the time to root it out once and for all is *now*. To help you along, I've listed nine ways you can creatively and ethically borrow ideas.

> *Ask for help. Let me repeat: Ask for help.*

1. Ask for help

Let me repeat. Ask for help. You would be surprised how eager other people might be to help you out. For example, the highly successful head of a large military personnel office arranges for her top people to visit the personnel offices of some of America's largest and most dynamic corporations. Insights and ideas the staff gains prompt creative solutions to problems. All she had to do was ask (Linden, *From Vision to Reality*). Of course, you should be prepared to return the favor and not to seek to get something for nothing.

2. Become your competition's customer

Do your competitors keep mailing lists? Do they send out promotional mail or newsletters? Are *you* on their lists? I'm serious. You should receive your competition's promotional mail. That way, you'll keep up with their new ideas and sales strategies.

This device works in the public sector as well. Several of the government innovators cited in Linden's book took steps to find out the nature of similar services offered by "competing" organizations. Only by knowing what the competition was up to could these agencies evaluate the quality of their own services and products.

Examining how your best competitors operate and manage their businesses is sometimes easier than analyzing your own operation. For example, it's certainly easier to be objective when looking at what someone else does. Obtaining your competitor's performance numbers on production, cost, quality, and speed, and then understanding how these results were achieved is known widely as "benchmarking." The purpose of benchmarking is not to set your own performance targets but to get outside your organization's own assumptions and habits to see patterns of success.

3. Start a Borrow File

Whenever you see an ad, a direct mail piece, a quote, a passage in a book, or a comic strip that makes you see things in a different way, clip it out and put it in your Borrow File. Periodically review your Borrow File in search of new angles or new ways of approaching old problems.

4. Announce a "Not-Invented-Here" contest

To encourage those around you to get out of the rut caused by the NIH syndrome, start a "Not-Invented-Here" contest. Have people submit ideas borrowed from various sources. You might include the following prize categories:

Most Easily Implementable Idea

Best Idea from a Family Member

Best Idea from a Foreign Company

Best Idea from a Friend

Best Idea from a Competitor

Best Idea Obtained by Asking for Help

5. Become a part of the marketplace

Sony demands that their research-and-development people and marketers spend 25 percent of their time out of the office in the marketplace of the consumer. This policy has paid handsome dividends. A Sony engineer was watching the growing trend of California's youth going up and down the California coast on roller skates . . . alone. The engineer put two and two together. Youth . . . alone . . . on wheels . . . with hands occupied. Youth . . . music. Fast-forward to: the Walkman.

6. Identify, visit, and experience top quality

Is your organization absolutely the best? Is no one out there in the world doing a better job than your organization does? If you answer yes to these questions, then you're missing out on real opportunities. By recognizing the overwhelming odds that somebody, somewhere, is doing what you do, or part of what you do, a little bit better than you are, you can seek out those people or those operations, visit them, and spot wonderful ideas that you otherwise might not think about.

I recently conducted a Creativity Workshop at the Ritz-Carlton in Washington, D.C. As I was checking in, I noticed that the front desk clerk referred to me by name. As I entered my room, I found the *TV Guide* opened to that day's date. During my workshop, I asked the hotel staff for masking tape. It arrived in three minutes. Then, at dinner that evening, I noticed the crest of the Ritz on the china plates, all properly facing each diner. And it hit me: quality isn't a *program*, with a beginning, a middle, and surely an end, but a *mind-set*. In this age of *programs* lasting only three months, the notion of a *frame of mind* becomes crucial for those organizations truly seeking quality *and* creativity as a way of organizational life.

> *Visit and experience top quality. A field trip to a successful and original grocery store helped executives in a completely different line of work come up with great ideas.*

You can use this technique of visiting and experiencing quality and apply it to operations wholly unconnected with yours. While teaching at a state government agency in Richmond, Virginia, I took a group of executives on a "field trip." To their surprise, we visited Ukrops Grocery Store, a highly successful operation in Richmond. Ukrops is closed on Sundays, doesn't sell alcohol, employs senior citizens as baggers, carries your grocery bags to the car, and believes that the customer is king.

I divided my class of executives into small groups of four. Each group was charged with identifying an agency problem, walking around Ukrops for thirty minutes, buying one item, returning to class, and coming up with some ideas to help solve the problem.

The insights they gained from experiencing top quality were easily transferable as great ideas for their own managerial problems, which had absolutely nothing to do with grocery stores.

7. *Read a biography of a person you're trying to emulate*

As you're sitting at your desk stuck on a talk you have to give tomorrow, think how creative it would be to have Thomas Jefferson take over your assignment for a while. Although you can't call up Manpower and request a day of Jefferson's services, you can do the next best thing by reading biographies of great and inspirational people. Try such topics as history, philosophy, politics, science, and sports.

8. Start a clipping file or subscribe to a computer clipping service

To stay ahead of the pack, you don't have to roam through volumes of information at the library or wait for your associate to clip an article for you. Your competition is taking advantage of the almost one thousand on-line data bases with their thousands of choices all accessible to the public via a common on-line service such as Dialog, Western Union, BRS Information Technologies, and CompuServe (see Resources).

A full listing of all available data bases with descriptions may be obtained in the following directories: *Directory of Online Databases* and *Computer Readable Databases* (see Resources).

An excellent data base for people dealing with community problems is the *Community Action Network* (CAN). The CAN catalog describes more than seven hundred concrete solutions in twenty problem categories ranging from AIDS to alcohol abuse to teenage suicide to unemployment (see Resources).

By finding out what other people are doing in particular areas, you can discover great ideas. They won't be your ideas. But they will be great ideas just waiting for you to do something with them. You can even network with other inventors and innovators. The National Network of Innovators offers a computer bulletin board that inventors can access through their own computers (see Resources).

9. If at first you don't succeed, take a break!

When you sit down to solve a problem all by yourself, when you sit at your desk determined to come up with some innovative solutions, often you fail. Instead of trying and trying and trying again, take a break! Recognize that creativity does not come just from your insides, but from the outside as well. A scene, a sound, an odd object can give you that idea you've been looking for.

If those surroundings aren't producing anything, then change them, and take a break. One midlevel manager at Philip Morris leaves his office and takes a walk down by the river. The change of scenery often sparks the thought he was seeking.

When I need ideas, I'll often sit down and watch some mindless TV. My premeditated goal is to come up with ideas I can use. This "focused observation" has worked wonders for me on many occasions. Sometimes I even take a problem with me to the golf course. I then look for ideas in the context of greens, sand traps, fairways, divots, tees, birdies, bogeys, and pars.

Chapter 12

MUSIC OF THE HEMISPHERES
Overcoming Mental Blocks

Has this ever happened to you?

You're at a party talking to a small group of people. A friend walks up. You want to introduce her, but your mind goes blank. You can't remember her name!

You're in a heated debate with your boss. Just when you're about to make the winning point, your mind goes blank. You can't think of a thing, even though you can "feel" the argument you were about to make.

You're writing an important report. As you turn to the next blank page, your mind goes blank as well. Words won't come, even though you had a feeling about what you wanted to say.

It never fails, of course—after your embarrassed friend leaves or your boss wins the argument or your report misses its deadline—you remember your friend's name, you know those winning arguments like the back of your hand, and your report writes itself in your mind. Good old 20/20 hindsight. We're all blessed with that ability to know what we should have done. But we're not as well endowed with the knowledge of what to do when the mental block occurs.

A mental block usually crops up when you seek an immediate answer in a direct, linear way, yet your brain needs time to free-associate for the solution. If you were to equate your brain with a telecommunications system, its capacity could be likened to the total number of phone circuits in the world multiplied fourteen hundred times. With this vast

Blocks occur when you demand a direct, immediate answer from yourself, yet you need freedom to find a different kind of answer.

array of interconnected lines, your plea for a direct answer is often met with a busy signal. To get your answer, you need to make the call on an open line, one of the many in your mind. For some reason, however, we seem to pick the line already jammed with other calls. We need ways to find that open line.

Metaphors Left and Right

To Plato, the brain was a block of wax. In his words: "Imagine a block of wax with thoughts imprinted into it." To Aristotle, the brain cooled the blood, while thinking took place in the heart. In more modern times, we tend to think of the brain as a giant computer, complete with input, output, programs, and the equivalent of circuit boards.

A good example of left-brain thinking is balancing your checkbook. The "high" comes from reconciling the numbers.

Most images we use today to describe creativity and the work of the brain rely heavily on the increasingly familiar divisions of function between the "left brain" and "right brain." The left and right hemispheres of the brain, researchers have found in many studies, process information in contrasting ways; they retain individual styles of thinking while still managing to work in a complementary way.

As many readers already will know, the left hemisphere specializes in verbal, logical, and analytical thinking. Its favored way of thinking is linear: first things first. It excels in the three R's: reading, writing, and arithmetic. An apt example of left-brain thinking is balancing your checkbook. The "high" comes from reconciling the numbers.

The right hemisphere specializes in nonverbal, visual, spatial, and perceptual thinking. Its favored way of thinking is nonlinear and relies on simultaneous information processing. It excels at seeing patterns and relationships and is undaunted by ambiguity and paradoxes. An apt example of right-brain thinking is highway driving. Successful driving requires the skill of simultaneously processing divergent visual and other perceptual information. The "high" comes from all of the free association that goes on in your mind while driving without conscious monitoring. How often have you driven a familiar route and suddenly realized that you don't really remember passing a particular scene or noteworthy milepost?

The left and right sides share and communicate their views by way of a nerve bundle called the *corpus callosum*. Throughout the day, the two sides work cooperatively. In musical activities, the left side reads the music and keeps the beat while the right side handles tone, melody, and expression.

In the creative process, the left side is basically "fact friendly," the right side more "idea friendly." We need both sides interacting in a complementary way to come up with creative solutions to problems:

Left Side of Brain   **Right Side of Brain**

Defining the problem

Gathering information [READY]

Analyzing information

Incubating information

Free-associating [FIRE]

Intuitive flash

Evaluating possible solution [AIM]

Implementing solution

You can readily see how these left-right brain functions reflect our "Ready, Fire . . . Aim!" model of creative thinking. Getting ready and defining the problem is basically a left-brain exercise. Using one of the many idea-generating techniques described in earlier chapters—firing off in divergent directions in the brainstorming process—is a right-brain exercise. And aiming and choosing a solution is another left-brain exercise, informed now, however, by the right brain.

The following chart should help put many of these left/right functions into better perspective:

Information Processing in the Brain

	Left Side of Brain	Right Side of Brain
Historical Perspective	Yang	Yin
	Ego	Id
	Conscious	Unconscious
	Mind	Body
Information Gathering	Thinking	Feeling
	Sensing	Intuition
Remembering	Words	Images
	Numbers	Patterns
	Parts	Wholes
	Names	Faces
Expressing	Verbal	Nonverbal
	Talking	Dreams, gestures, gut feelings
	Counting	Drawing, singing
	Writing	Doodling
Thinking	Analytical	Visionary
	Linear	Spatial
	Logical	Analogical
	Rational	Free association
	Sequential	Simultaneous
	Vertical	Lateral
	Convergent	Divergent
	Deductive	Inductive
Choosing	Black/White	Gray
Performance	Trying	Reflex
	Execution	Visualization
Management	Rules, procedures	Shared vision
Organization	Capital	Values
	People	Commitment
	Raw Materials	Ideas
	Technology	Innovation

Hemispheres and the Body

Neurophysiological research shows that at birth the hemispheres are separate but equal: if one is damaged in infancy, the other hemisphere can take over all its functions and the child will grow up with normal abilities. This capability is called *plasticity* of the brain. However, by age seven, the two hemispheres have specialized, and injury to the left hemisphere will adversely affect the verbal abilities and the control of the right side of the body. Injury to the right hemisphere will diminish spatial abilities and the control of the left side of the body. Thus, with specialization, each hemisphere becomes responsible for control of the *opposite* side of the body.

Hemispheres and Mental Blocks

So how do we relate this hemispheric control to the process of overcoming a mental block? Simple. Basically, if you're stuck, try using your *other* hand.

If you're bogged down in a problem and need a jump start, start scribbling with a pencil in your *other* hand or pick up a small object with your *other* hand. The unfamiliar muscular movements from the nondominant side of your body will trigger electrical flow in the nondominant side of your brain. The net result? New connections—a new perspective—possibly a new idea.

If you're a bit skeptical after reading this section—well, I was too, until I began to use this technique in my creativity workshops. My workshop participants, so far, all report significant changes in the way they view routine problems and significant increases in the quantity and quality of their proposed solutions to those problems, after using the "nondominant" technique.

So get ready. I'm about to teach you to pay attention to which nostril you are now favoring when you inhale and exhale.

Triggering the Opposite Side of Your Brain

What I encourage you to do is to try some exercises that make you feel distinctly uncomfortable: using your nondominant side to make the nondominant side of your brain do things it normally doesn't do. By making that side of your brain control some motor functions, you'll also prompt your entire brain to look at things in different, creative ways.

Step One

Take out a sheet of paper and, using your dominant hand, write down six words that describe you.

Step Two

Take your pencil out of your hand and for one minute focus your eyes on the center of this graphic mandala.

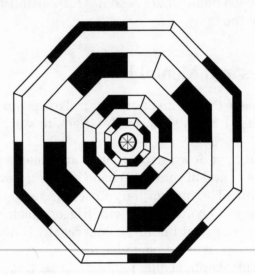

Step Three

Now, using your opposite hand, write down six different words that describe you. Be a kid again! Draw them all over a sheet of paper, not one on top of the other.

Step Four

What similarities and differences do you see between the two sets of words?

The Power of Your Other Hand

Answering a question with your nondominant hand is a proven counseling technique used to bring out childhood and emotional issues.

Most people write opposite responses with their two hands. By "opposite," I mean *work vs. home settings, analytical vs. emotional traits, adult vs. child experiences*, or *strong vs. vulnerable feelings*.

Many executives now use this technique to find out their emotional response to a question. It definitely triggers in you the ability to see answers that normally would not have surfaced. To get these opposite thoughts, you don't have to be writing with your nondominant hand; you could use your nondominant hand to wash yourself in the shower—which could be fun even if you don't come up with new ideas.

> *Stuck? Try using your other hand.*

The mandala also helped you to trigger opposite thoughts by taking you on a spatial journey in and out of the design. Focusing on the center of the mandala or on any stationary object is an excellent form of stress reduction.

Historically, the two biggest proponents of using your other hand for additional answers were Leonardo da Vinci and Benjamin Franklin.

Let's Try Both Hands

To get some practice finding answers with your "other" hand, apply the steps given on the previous page to a specific question or problem. Write down answers or comments using your normal writing hand, then relax for a minute with the mandala, then write answers—all over the page— with your "other" hand. What similarities and differences do you see between your two sets of answers?

Determining Your Brain/Body Dominance

Our hands are only one body part that can help us overcome a mental block. Let's take a trip from our eyes to our feet to determine the dominance or nondominance of other pairs of body parts or of various sides of one body part. Once you know the dominant way that you move, all you need to do to break out of your mental block is to activate a nondominant body part.

Eyes

Most of us think that we focus on an object with both of our eyes. Actually we use just one eye to focus on what we're doing or reading. To determine which eye is dominant, simply hold your thumb at arm's length out in front of you and use your thumb to block out a small object on a far wall such as a light switch or corner of a picture frame. Do this with both eyes open. When the light switch is blocked out, then close your *right* eye. If your thumb is still blocking out the light switch, then it was your *left* eye that was dominant in focusing. If the light switch "moved," as it will for 50 percent of you now reading this book, then you focused on it with your *right* eye. On page 142 is a chart for you to keep score on the various more-dominant parts or sides of your body.

Determining which eye is dominant, for example, has become very beneficial for athletes, for it has been shown that right-handed batters with a dominant left eye have a significantly higher batting average—they don't have to turn their heads to see the ball! The same increased batting statistic is true for left-handed batters with dominant right eyes. One basketball coach told me about the dramatic improvement his team made in free-throw shooting when players determined their dominant eyes. It turns out that his worst shooters were setting up the ball before shooting in front of their dominant eyes, thus throwing off the spatial location of the basket.

Wink

Wink one eye, then the other. Does one feel more natural to wink? If so, that's your dominant eye for winking. Don't worry if this eye is not the one you use for focusing. Mark down your dominance.

Smile

Smile at yourself while looking in a mirror. Which side of your mouth goes higher? If you can't tell, look for which side of your face has more wrinkles. The higher, more wrinkled side is your dominant one. Mark down your dominance.

Arms

Cross your arms with one arm on top of the other. Whichever one is on top is your dominant arm. Mark down your dominance.

Thumbs

Bring your hands together, interlocking your fingers, making sure you have one thumb on top of the other. Whichever thumb is on top is your dominant thumb. Now, separate your hands and bring them back together with the other thumb on top. Feels awkward, doesn't it? Mark down your dominance.

You're probably starting to see that not only do we do things in a dominant, patterned way, but we are also a mixture of right- and left-side dominances.

Hands

Eleven percent of the population is left-handed, so mark down which hand you use for writing. If you were switched in grade school from left to right, you are still to be considered left-handed.

Legs

Cross your legs at the knee. Which leg feels more comfortable on top? That's your dominant leg—mark it down.

Feet

If I rolled a ball to you, which foot would you use to kick it? That's your dominant foot—mark it down.

Thoughts

This exercise will require help from another person. Ask a friend to ask you a question. Then tell the friend to observe whether your eyes move to the left or the right as you contemplate the answer. Do not have the friend stare at you and don't stare back. Your eyes need to be relaxed to move. If your eyes go up or down before they go to the side, that's natural. Your eyes normally go up when you are visualizing an answer to a question like "What was I wearing last Tuesday?" Your eyes normally go down when you are *feeling* an answer to a question like "Was the ocean real cold that day?" If your eyes don't move to one side or the other, allow yourself to be observed later at a more spontaneous time. Mark down whether your eyes moved to the right or to the left.

Visualization

Close your eyes. Now visualize a circular wall clock on the wall in front of you. Reach out and take the clock off the wall and put it on the front of your face. Now put one finger of one hand at twelve o'clock and one finger of the other hand at three o'clock. Open your eyes and note if three o'clock is on the right or left side of your face; mark down which side.

Mixed Dominance

If you saw the clock both ways on your face or if neither leg feels more or less comfortable when crossed on top of the other, then your dominance for that part of your body is mixed. On the chart, you can check both right and left sides.

Scoring Your Dominance

Count up the number of left- and right-side dominances. The usual score I've seen in my workshops is seven for the right side and three for the left. These body dominances then show the exact opposite brain dominance, because the left side of the body is controlled by the right side of the brain and vice versa. So if your body score is seven right-side and three left, then your brain dominance profile is seven left-side and three right.

Brain and Body Dominance Chart

Left Side of Body	Right Side of Body
☐ Eyes	☐ Eyes
☐ Wink	☐ Wink
☐ Smile	☐ Smile
☐ Arms	☐ Arms
☐ Thumbs	☐ Thumbs
☐ Hands	☐ Hands
☐ Crossed legs	☐ Crossed legs
☐ Feet	☐ Feet
☐ Thoughts	☐ Thoughts
☐ Visualization	☐ Visualization
[ ]	[ ]
Right Brain	**Left Brain**

Overcoming Mental Blocks

The next time you feel stuck and want a fresh beginning, just cross your arms or legs in the nondominant way. When you're looking at a magazine, instead of browsing through the pages from left to right, go from right to left.

When going to the movie theater, you'll usually want to sit on the right side of the theater if your left eye is dominant, and on the left side if your right eye is dominant. This might explain the proverbial argument you and your spouse or date have when deciding where to sit, especially if it's true, as some people think, that couples tend to have complementary or offsetting patterns of brain/body dominance. To exercise the nondominant side of your brain, sit on the side you least prefer.

If you play tennis and want to play in what many athletes call "the zone," then you need to be able to trigger the right side of the brain to assist you with the spatial concepts needed for success in tennis and most other sports. Between each point, just focus on your tennis racket strings. The spatial exercise of looking at the strings will trigger the right spatial side of your brain, will help eliminate distracting sounds from the audience, and will actually make the ball look bigger and slower.

This One's Really Healthful

You might also try the walk-a-mile-for-an-idea approach to overcoming mental blocks. Einstein walked a lot to help solve his problems. He sometimes grew so involved in thought that he would become lost in his own town of Princeton, New Jersey.

According to the codirector of the Walking Center in New York City, "There is a very dynamic action involving both sides of the brain when walking, and you tend to become more creative." Fast walking seems to help jog the memory of forgetful adults, according to a study conducted by Dr. Robert Dustman of the Salt Lake City Veterans Administration Medical Center. And Dr. Ted Bashore of the Medical College of Pennsylvania believes that aerobic exercise will speed up the brain's ability to process information.

This One's Fairly Weird

Pause for a minute and breathe only through your nose. If you'll pay really close attention to your breathing, you'll be able to figure out that you're favoring one of your nostrils over the other. To confirm which nostril is dominant (having more air going through it), close off one nostril and breathe. Then close off the other and breathe. When you figure out which one is now dominant, take your finger and close off that nostril. Feels strange, doesn't it?

> *Which side of the movie theater do you tend to prefer . . . and through which nostril are you breathing?*

I know you probably have better things to do, but several times today, pause for a minute and notice which nostril you're favoring in your breathing. Research shows that you will favor one nostril over the other for about ninety minutes and then switch to the other. This subtle rhythm was discovered more than five thousand years ago and is just one of our body's many ultradian rhythms: short cycles found in metabolic functions and perceptual abilities.

Recent research has shown that you can tell which side of your brain is dominant at any given time by observing which nostril you're favoring in your breathing. Right nostril dominance shows left brain activity; left nostril dominance shows right brain activity.

You know what's coming, don't you? Yes, research further shows that you can trigger the nondominant side of your brain by closing off your dominant nostril and breathing through your nondominant side for up to five minutes. The dominance switches every ninety minutes naturally, but you can spark the nondominant side with this exercise. You will not change the ninety-minute cycle, however.

I use the technique all the time. While sitting at my desk in need of a right-brain infusion, I close off my right nostril and breathe through my left nostril. Voilà! Naturally, I keep my finger discreetly on the *outside* of my nostril and try to look like I'm just leaning on my nose.

I'm not alone in my use of nondominant parts or sides to get the nondominant side of my brain working or to get a particular side of the brain working. I know some professional athletes who use the nose technique between golf shots or before skiing down the big slope. I even had a physician tell me he's using the device as a sleeping aid. When he has trouble falling asleep because of an overactive brain, he breathes only through his left nostril to trigger the right side of his brain. The right side, if you'll recall, is nonjudging and more dreamlike. I have borrowed the technique myself and can attest to its validity. It certainly beats counting sheep.

These Can Help in the Long Run

If you're left- or right-brain dominant, there are specific things you can do that will help you achieve balance, depending on which side you favor. Visconti 2000, the Center for Peak Performance and Neuro-Sensory Development, recommends ongoing activities and routines that can bring out the potential of your lesser-used, nondominant side.

You right-brain types, go balance your checkbooks; if left-brain dominant, fly a kite.

For example, if you're left-brain dominant, Visconti 2000 recommends:

> *Kite flying*
> *Learning to dance*
> *Playing Frisbee*
> *Learning to sail*
> *Singing lessons*
> *Joining a choir*
> *Public speaking*
> *Taking a course in storytelling*
> *Finding a way to be with children*
>   *(become a Big Sister or Big Brother)*
> *Volunteering in a children's hospital*
> *Drawing and painting*
> *Using colored pencils/pens in note taking*

If you're right-brain dominant:

> *Make miniature models*
> *Start a stamp or coin collection*
> *Keep daily checkbook balances (to the penny!)*
> *Keep dated records of activities*
> *Join competitive swimming, running, or bicycling (where you*
>   *have to be conscious of time)*
> *Play golf*
> *Read history books or novels*
> *Join a history discussion group*
> *Ballroom dancing*

Learn chess
Paint (by numbers!)
Take a course in auto repair or financial investments
Chart the stock market
Learn a foreign language
Visit a science museum
Start an insect identification collection
Write, type, and file your ideas
Keep organized files of bills, correspondence

This One's Really High-Tech

Let's face it. We can learn all of the creativity techniques in the world, but our mind will sometimes get stuck in a rut. We just can't get our brain in sync.

Don't give up. Borrow an idea from the latest brain research, which shows that nonverbal audio patterns have a dramatic effect on consciousness. According to Bob Monroe, founder of the internationally known Monroe Institute, certain sound patterns when blended and sequenced together can gently lead your brain into relaxation, sleep, concentration, or heightened creativity. Using stereo headphones, Monroe sends separate sound pulses to each ear, prompting the two hemispheres of the brain to act in unison to "hear" a third signal—not an actual sound, but an electrical signal created by both brain hemispheres working together simultaneously. This coherent brain state is known as hemispheric synchronization, or "Hemi-Sync." While this brain synchronization occurs naturally in everyday life, unfortunately it typically exists only for random, brief periods of time. The Hemi-Sync audio technologies developed by the Monroe Institute are designed to assist you in achieving and sustaining this highly productive brain state.

Using results from more than thirty years of research into the effects of sound on human consciousness, the Monroe Institute makes Hemi-Sync technology available to the public in a number of ways, including intensive training programs for exploration and development of expanded states of consciousness. The institute offers numerous audiocassette programs, dealing with accelerated learning, stress reduction, pain control, sleep enhancement, and (my favorite) heightened creativity. Also available is Explorer I, a new Hemi-Sync–emitting device designed to facilitate a range of desired states of consciousness.

A related research area is psychoacoustics—the relationship between musical styles and specific emotions. To achieve an audio environment conducive to new ideas, I recommend that you choose music following these guidelines:

1. Avoid music with lyrics. Classical, light jazz, and New Age are acceptable.
2. Avoid music that demands your attention.
3. Avoid music with large, sudden changes in amplitude. Punk rock is out.
4. Use music with sustained tones and subtle variations.

Some recommendations:
Brahms: Concerto in A Minor, Op. 102
Chopin: Piano Concerto No. 1 in E Minor, Op. 11
Beethoven: Sonata No. 14 in C-Sharp Minor, Op. 27
Vivaldi: L'Estro Armonico, Op. 2; Concerto No. 5 in A Major

In a small sample size, I have noticed that many computer programmers prefer hard rock music while program coding. Joel Smith, a Macintosh programmer, states that jazz and New Age music cut off his coding creativity, but Aerosmith, AC/DC, Van Halen—and Beethoven's Ninth—work wonders.

Blockbusters

Mental blocks are natural in the creative process. Now you know some quick and efficient ways to overcome them. To help you further, I've prepared the following When-You're-Stuck Action Sheet.

When-You're-Stuck

Here's all you have to do to get a lift from both sides of your brain:

Use Your Nondominant Body Parts

Cross your legs the wrong way.

Interlock your fingers the wrong way.

Use your nondominant eye to read a short magazine article.

Write down some thoughts with your "other" hand.

Breathe through your left nostril for a right-brain jolt.

Breathe through your right nostril for a left-brain jolt.

Doodle or scribble with the "wrong" hand.

Do Things in a Strange Way or Do Some Strange Things

Drive to work a different way.

Close your eyes and daydream about your ideal vacation spot.

Make a short phone call to a friend and just catch up.

Browse through a magazine and just look at the pictures.

Walk around and pretend that you have to get something.

Take a shower and sing the *Hallelujah Chorus*.

Do a crossword puzzle.

While pretending to analyze a spreadsheet on your computer, play a computer game.

Read a report that's been sitting on your desk for a month.

Manipulate Your Time

Write down your thoughts as fast as you can. Then go back and edit.

Set a specific time limit for completing your task.

Divide your task into "doable" chunks and tackle them one by one.

Idea Map your problem and rapidly rank the ideas you generate.

Use an opposite Idea Map by answering this question: What would I *never* do to solve this problem?

CONCLUSION

All four of the steps that form this book involve ways of removing obstacles to the realization of ideas. In cultivating creative *freedom*, the Idea Person removes the blinders that may have prevented the generation of multiple ideas (as opposed to the "right" idea) and disarms the power of negative assumptions. In practicing *expression*, exercises such as Idea Maps, by their very form, go beyond the obstacles presented by habitual, circumscribed, linear ways of thinking.

The obstacle to *creation* is, in a sense, reality itself—i.e., "reality" as we assume it to be. The Idea Person does not accept this reality, even though he or she may be, and preferably is, highly realistic. The creative person "escapes" into *other* realities—worlds where the future happens right now, where everything turns into its opposite, where the things we believe are true just aren't, where the normal point of view is abandoned, everything is metaphorical, we trespass into other people's brains and flip-flop our own. And the very successful Idea People make this escape for the same reason that kids play or that other grown-ups read novels or go to the movies—for the sheer joy of the trip. For the fun of it—and all the rewards simply follow.

Creation assumes reality to be plastic and transformable and generates ideas for new and, we hope, better ways that this reality can bend. The next step involves the process of finding out if reality will.

The Fourth Step

Because *action* is the step of the creative process least often associated with imagination and invention, it lends itself especially well to application of these attributes. *Action*—the phase of bringing ideas into reality—requires great ideas to match the ideas being enacted.

Action is the stage of the creative process where innovation meets organization—meets production—meets sales—meets distribution. We need to bring innovation into every step, in order to give it a chance—if our ideas and our organizations are to thrive in the competitive world of the 1990s and beyond.

The creative process is global, in every sense. This is not the machine age, where lockstep production and distribution could (if indeed it ever could) just grind out the products of the mind. More and more, every step of the way must be a product of the mind—the open mind, free to imagine, able to feel, empowered to create.

The following chapters help you create and maintain an openness to ideas, within the organization, in your own routines, in meetings, in your home. The purpose: to help your great ideas fulfill their creator's intentions. To bring worthy ideas all the way through the cycle of physical realization is, by another name, *fulfillment*.

Chapter 13

THE GARDEN OF GREATNESS
Fostering an Openness to Ideas

So you've got great ideas. Now it's time to figure out how to convince others in your organization (or in your marketplace) that the ideas are indeed great and worthy of their investment of time, money, or other resources. To do that, to sell your ideas to others, you must first analyze your organization's receptiveness to new ideas. Is your organization eager for the new and the different? Or does it tend to cling to the old ways of doing things?

I believe that you can think about the openness of an organization to new ideas by considering the following formula:

$$\text{Openness} = \frac{\text{\# Ideas} \times (\text{\# Implemented} + \text{Fast Failures}) \times \text{Shared Vision}}{\text{Penalty for Failure}}$$

If you will remember your high school algebra, you will see that you can increase the degree of openness in an organization by increasing the fraction's numerator or by decreasing the denominator. Thus to increase the numerator (thereby increasing openness) you should seek to increase the quantity of ideas generated, increase the fast failures, and create a common and agreed-on vision. Simultaneously, to decrease the denominator (thereby increasing openness) you should seek to reduce the penalty for failure.

Reducing the Penalty for Failure

Here's the cardinal rule of thumb for fostering an openness to new ideas in any organization or in any individual: Make sure that the penalty for failure is not greater than the penalty for doing nothing.

To reduce the perception of a penalty for failure, Du Pont's Textile Fibers Division actually rewards failures with a quarterly failure trophy. The failed efforts must have been ethically sound, recognized as failures quickly, and learned from thoroughly. In *From Vision to Reality*, Linden points out that a common trait among the successful innovators he studied was a willingness by the managers to accept failure by subordinates. Indeed, there was an *expectation* that people would make mistakes.

Increasing "Fast Failures"

Many people dream of success. To me, success can only be achieved through repeated failure and introspection. In fact, success represents the one percent of your work which results only from the ninety-nine percent that is called failure.
—*Soichiro Honda, Founder, Honda Motors*

An organization that is open to creativity accepts failure. Indeed, the organization that is open to creativity expects failure. It wants failure. For if failure is not taking place, neither is innovation. At first, "expecting failure" might sound counterproductive. After all, failure means a loss of money (your money), self-esteem (your self-esteem), and status (your status). You might wonder, "But I've spent my career learning to win, not fail."

Perhaps a new image of "failure" is needed. Mr. Honda referred to the "ninety-nine percent [of work] that is called failure." What we call failure might merely be stark evidence of the creative process at work. Perhaps we should look at failure as our best teacher, much like that memorable teacher we all had in school, the one who said, "No, that's not the right answer; have you considered this?" Perhaps we should look at failure as a learning process, as the taking of a course. Small failures characterize the course; great ideas stand waiting as the diploma.

When Bill Gore, inventor of Gore-Tex, explained to me that he wanted a new use for Gore-Tex every week, he also set the guideline for risk taking. He would say, "You can try anything, as long as it's above

CREATIVE RULE OF THUMB #16

Make sure that the penalty for failure is not greater than the penalty for doing nothing.

the waterline. If you want to drill holes below the waterline, you need to check with your sponsor [boss]." Thus anything goes. We expect failure. Do anything but jeopardize the health of the organization.

Paul MacCready, the aerodynamics wizard who invented the human-powered *Gossamer Condor*, credits his success to crude, fast, and inexpensive experimentation. That is, fast failure. "You need to test it easily, be able to run along with it, and catch it. If a tube breaks [on the airplane], you can crudely fix it with a broom handle."

If failure is to take place, the innovator wants it to occur fast so that time and money are not unnecessarily wasted. To speed up the failures, the successful innovator will initiate small-scale tests of new ideas, conduct personal surveys to determine the effectiveness of ideas, and always remain open to critical feedback. To get started on the path of increasing fast failures, you might first consider replacing the word "failure" with "glitch," "false start," "course correction," or more positively, "new insight."

In my video company, we tried to be the first to produce videos on current health topics such as AIDS, herpes, cocaine, and steroids. *The Wall Street Journal* even called us, humorously, "ambulance-chasing cartoonists," because we were always the first to market and schools would call us up with suggestions for videos on new health topics. Because we were first, many of our video distributors would say that our new video would never sell. To prove them wrong, my company would send out our own direct mail advertising to school systems.

However, before committing to a large direct mail effort, costing thousands of dollars, we always sought a "fast failure." I followed the advice of a major advertising executive who urged me to refrain from printing a hundred thousand pieces of a four-color print run. Instead, he counseled, print only five hundred in black and white, mail them to yourself and your sales force, to your office staff and your spouse, and to a small sampling of your customers. Then call them and find out whether the promotional effort was a success or a "fast failure."

Achieving a Shared Vision

Think back to a time when you were totally absorbed by an activity, so absorbed that you completely forgot to eat. Was it structuring a new deal, learning a new computer program, designing a new system, or playing with your child?

These hyperproductive experiences, called "flow states" by psychologist Mihaly Csikszentmihalyi, are times of intensely focused consciousness. When a task is challenging and we have the necessary skill level to perform it, we will likely experience a flow state. This flow state is magnified by an increase in the level of challenge and the development or possession of the skills needed to meet the challenge. If an imbalance between the challenge and needed skills occurs, then the flow state disappears. Anxiety sets in when the challenge exceeds skill level, boredom when skill level exceeds challenge.

The forces producing a flow state, which in turn leads to vision, are depicted in the following figure:

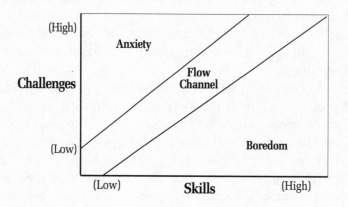

This simple model is an excellent way to show that we move in and out of our flow state throughout the day. As more work is piled on or as we attain new skills, we have to be aware that we will experience moments of anxiety and moments of boredom.

According to Csikszentmihalyi, the visionary leader is a person with a high level of skills who constantly seeks new challenges through "what if . . ." games. Vision results at the high end of flow state experiences. Thus, one way to achieve the desired vision is to maximize your time in the visionary flow state. Csikszentmihalyi, in his book *Flow: The Psychology of Optimal Experience. Steps Toward Enhancing the Quality of Life* (New York: Harper & Row, 1990), provides some concrete suggestions:

1. *Reduce the number of unnecessary meetings.*

2. *Set aside office time just for thinking.*

3. Don't be so worried about winning the game that you're too distracted to sink the shot.

4. Reduce the time devoted to "putting out fires."

Your vision, the one you seek to share in your organization, is a combination of your acquired knowledge, your instincts, and your dreams. When shared and accepted by your organization, your vision will serve as a great engine to innovation. When everyone knows the vision and heads in the same direction, the degree of successful innovation goes up. Such a vision will act as a bridge to the future. To bear the heavy load of change, that "vision-bridge" needs to be

1. Directed toward the future.

2. Usable today.

3. Firmly grounded in the past.

4. Stable yet flexible to changing environments.

5. Easily understood.

6. Well promoted.

Promoting the Vision

To promote that vision, and to make sure it is truly "shared," here are some suggestions you might consider for your organization.

1. Hang pictures of your vision

What I said earlier about designing your own office also applies to the larger office environment. For example, while Grumman Aerospace was working on the NASA moon mission, pictures of the moon were displayed all over their manufacturing operations.

2. Give feeling to your vision

Before filming *Ordinary People*, Robert Redford, the director, gathered his cinematographers together to listen to a recording of Pachelbel's Canon in D Major. He then asked them to create an opening suburban scene that related to the music.

3. Rename places and things to fit the vision

As previously mentioned, Apple Computer named its meeting rooms "Dorothy" and "Toto" to stress that there is a wizard in everyone. Du Pont calls its innovation team the "Oz" group; the members wear colorful, logo-enhanced T-shirts at training meetings.

4. Put a vision conversation piece on your desk

Applying another idea from the earlier suggestions for your own office, have everyone in your organization purchase a $5 desk ornament that conveys the meaning of the shared vision. John Guy, area sales manager for Hewlett-Packard, empowered every sales person to spend up to $25 for a desk item that communicates to them the vision of their yearly sales effort.

5. Help your people let go of the old vision

For many people, a new vision instills a feeling of loss. A common reaction to change is "We liked the way things were before." To help employees let go of these feelings, consider the following:

> What rituals have changed?
> Has the meaning of work changed?
> Is the perceived future going to be different?
> Will any employees feel incompetent working toward the new vision?
> Is control shifting to a new person or department?

6. Recognize that your organization will go through a "neutral zone" between the old reality and a new one

Work has an unreal sense about it and productivity is likely to break down with statements like "I just don't understand what the name of the game is anymore." Your "vision" becomes rapidly clear to your more intuitive employees. A clear plan of action and cost/benefit projection are necessary for your more analytical employees.

7. Celebrate new beginnings as they develop into new competencies and new relationships

New policies, procedures, and plans for the future will take time to become comfortable. To accelerate the process, build small-scale wins that produce visible results along the path to the shared vision.

Increasing the Number of New Ideas

After reducing the penalty for failure, increasing fast failures, and sharing your vision for the future, you should shift your focus toward increasing the number of ideas generated by your organization. Remember the first Creative Rule of Thumb: "The best way to come up with great ideas is to come up with lots of ideas and throw the bad ones away." A few organizational preparations should help foster an openness to creativity:

1. Make learning safe and fun

Offer training courses open to all, even family members.
Create break rooms with educational tools and toys.
Name your computers and other high-tech equipment to make them sound friendlier.
Provide laptop computers for home training.

2. Start an innovation team with projects such as

What paperwork can we cut?
How can we cut the number of approvals in half?
What rewards will motivate people?
How can we reduce harmful stress?

3. Fight Killer Phrases in meetings, reports, and conversations

Levy fines for Killer Phrases uttered or written.
Throw paper wads at Killer Phrase users.

4. Help participants in your meetings open up

Start meetings with one of the fun, divergent exercises found in the Great Idea Action Sheets in Chapter 16.
Give a break if meetings go longer than one hour.
Use short video segments to emphasize points.

And finally, to make yourself more open to great ideas, ask this question at the end of every workday:

What did I do different and better today from the way it was done when I came to work this morning?
                              —*Tom Peters,* Thriving on Chaos

Selling in the Organization

To help foster receptiveness to your new idea, you will need to communicate your vision to others, to sell them on the idea, to enlist their support and resources, and, indeed, to obtain their approval.

Doing What Everybody Else Does

Selling your idea requires communicating it. So look around. How does everybody else communicate ideas or suggest their adoption? They write memos, write reports, hold meetings, try pilot projects, do surveys. They do a host of things all involving the written or spoken word.

And what should you do when you try to sell your idea? Simple. Do what everybody else does. And then?

Do What Everybody Else Doesn't

When selling your ideas, your task is to be different, not for the sake of being different, but for the sake of successfully promoting your own great idea. If your target audience gets another report, another memo, another study, they will simply think it's just another idea. If your idea is truly a great idea, then it deserves a special promotional package.

In, Up, Down, and Out

Before we get to some concrete selling suggestions, let's consider the directions such selling might take. There are four: in, up, down, and out. First you must sell *in* or *inside*. That is, you must sell yourself on the quality of your own idea. Once you're truly convinced of the quality of your idea, you then must begin to sell *up* in the organization, *down* in the organization, and ultimately *outside* of the organization. These are *directions* your selling efforts can go, and the direction often determines the selling strategies you should adopt.

To see the direction I must follow to sell my new idea, I complete a Force Field Analysis. Using a chart like the one on the next page, I list the forces supporting and resisting my idea. The forces can be individuals, budget constraints, inertia, organizational climate, and many others.

Then I break down my strategy to see what I can do to encourage the supporting forces and neutralize or diminish the resisting forces.

After developing broad strategies, I look to see the four directions my promotional efforts should take: in, up, down, and out.

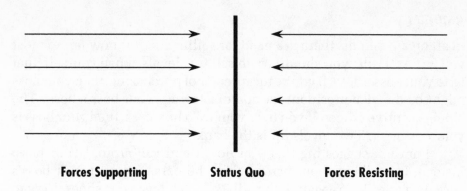

Forces Supporting   **Status Quo**   **Forces Resisting**

Selling In

Before you can possibly convince anyone else of the merits of your great idea, you must first sell yourself. You must gain your own absolute, unbending commitment to the quality of the idea. Put differently, you must fall in love with it. You must live your idea, follow it, use it, show it off to others—well before you begin to hype it inside and outside the organization.

After falling in love with your idea, you must also be prepared to fall out of love. Perhaps your idea has already been tried and improved on by someone else. If so, you should be ready to borrow their results and adapt. Overall, you should be aware that Idea Generators are notoriously optimistic. They are often blinded by their love for their own ideas and must learn to wake up to reality.

> *After falling in love with your idea, you must also be prepared to fall out of love.*

Linden, in *From Vision to Reality*, notes that the seven innovators studied all had a love affair with their visions. He described this common trait shared by the successful innovators this way:

> *Their personalities were similar in one respect: these seven individuals are clearly* driven *people. They approached their work and especially their initiatives with a tremendous focus, an energy level far beyond the norm. For some . . . this energy radiated outward in a very contagious way. Others . . . focused their energies more internally. Whether extravert or introvert, each of these innovators maintained a presence and a sense of drive that inevitably affected and infected those around them.*

Once you've developed and nurtured the necessary love, drive, and commitment to your idea, it's time to "radiate this energy" to others.

Selling Up

In all organizations, there is a need for selling up. But how far up must you go? As a rule, you should try to sell two levels above yourself, that is, to your boss's boss. If you're the director of purchasing, then your boss might be the vice president for manufacturing. Your boss's boss? The chief executive officer. If you own your own business, then your boss is your customer. Two levels up is the bank.

I am not suggesting that you do an end run around your boss. Instead, I'm talking about perspective, the perspective of your boss's boss. In a way, I'm repeating the advice to "change your shoes." Try to imagine how your boss's boss will react to your proposal. Thinking in this way will help you create a proposal that will "fly" up your organization.

Selling Down

Selling down requires selling two levels below your position, and to do this you'll have to "change your shoes," as suggested in Chapter 9. For once you've given your idea wings, it must be supported from below. Ideas from above often provoke cynicism because people below can't quite see your vision. To obtain the necessary "buy-in," you should consider some unique approaches:

Make your idea open for employee suggestions. Publish it in a newsletter and request reactions. Listen to how others think your idea will affect them. Then modify the idea if necessary.

Make your idea a part of the work environment. Visually portray your idea in photos or posters. Hang them on the walls of your office and meeting rooms.

Make employee participation possible. Assign implementation responsibilities to key staffers.

Selling Out

Some ideas are strictly internal ones that will never see the light of day outside the organization. Indeed, for inventions, trade secrets, or patents, the objective is *not* to sell outward but to keep such matters strictly confidential until the organization is ready to market them.

Other ideas, of course, must be sold outside the organization. To make your selling efforts truly creative, *creative* often means *different*. And being different requires you to . . . do what everybody else doesn't.

For example, to launch an upscale shopping mall along the river in New York City, one would hold a party, of course. And who does everybody else invite to the party? Why, all the bigwigs, all the politicos, all the VIPs.

And what did a truly creative development company do when it launched a new, upscale shopping mall along the river in New York?

It held a party and invited thousands of New York cabbies and their spouses. Can you imagine the ensuing free publicity to thousands of tourists asking the cabbies about new and different places?

> *To launch a new shopping mall in New York City, would you consider throwing a party—for cabdrivers?*

What does everybody else do to focus the nation's attention on a business magazine? They hire PR firms to plant stories in the nation's media. What did Malcolm Forbes do? Simple. He did what everybody else doesn't. He hired an exotic locale and threw himself a birthday party for a few million dollars that promptly turned into tens of millions of dollars worth of free *global* publicity. Most people don't have Malcolm Forbes's budget, so borrow the idea and adapt it to your promotional budget. You'll be amazed at some catchy ways you might attract the press for highly valuable publicity.

So check around your market. Look at your industry. Study your sector of government. See what everybody else does. Then you know what to do. At least seven things:

1. *Envision the future.*

2. *Ask, "What's the opposite?"*

3. *Challenge assumptions.*

4. *Change your shoes.*

5. *Create a metaphor.*

6. *Borrow and adapt.*

7. *Get out your colored pens and draw some Idea Maps.*

Sell the way you create—the way you created what you're selling. That way, you're always drawing energy from the source of the idea, and that energy puts a shine on anything you do. Creativity as an approach enriches every phase of life, and speeds the acceptance of the very ideas it produced in the first place.

How to Kill Your Idea

One of the best ways to sum up the actions you need to take on behalf of your idea is, of course, to consider the things you can do to undercut it. Here's my list of the top ten:

1. *Expect to receive all of the credit.*

2. *Never look for a second right answer.*

3. *Drag your feet, lack a sense of commitment.*

4. *Run it through a committee.*

5. *Wait for full analysis and market surveys.*

6. *Hold lengthy meetings to explore its merit.*

7. *Boost cost estimates just to be safe.*

8. *Set unrealistic, false deadlines.*

9. *Don't get views from other stakeholders.*

10. *Make sure it's the only idea you ever have.*

Selling Your Ideas

Once you determine who is supporting and resisting your idea, you will develop a sales strategy for communication in, up, down, and outside your organization.

Step 1 Describe your idea.

Step 2 Complete a Force Field Analysis.

List on the arrows the forces supporting and resisting your idea. For example, stakeholder support or opposition, budget constraints, inertia, organizational climate, and so on.

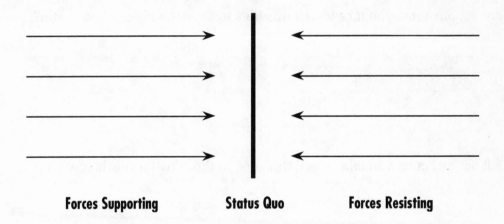

Forces Supporting   **Status Quo**   **Forces Resisting**

Step 3 Develop a broad sales strategy.

What can you do to encourage the supporting forces?

What can you do to neutralize or diminish the resisting forces?

Step 4 Develop sales efforts in, up, down, and outside your organization.

| **What Everybody Does** | **What Everybody Doesn't Do** |

What other actions must you take to sell yourself completely on this idea?

1. _____   1. _____

2. _____   2. _____

3. _____   3. _____

What actions must you take to sell this idea to those two levels above you?

1. _____   1. _____

2. _____   2. _____

3. _____   3. _____

What actions must you take to sell this idea to those two levels below you?

1. _____   1. _____

2. _____   2. _____

3. _____   3. _____

What actions must you take to sell this idea to those outside your organization?

1. _____   1. _____

2. _____   2. _____

3. _____   3. _____

Chapter 14

ON A SCALE FROM 1 TO GREAT

Evaluating New Ideas

It is by intuition that we discover and by logic that we prove.
—Henri Poincaré, Mathematician

Now that you know new ways to develop ideas, ideas will begin to come more easily and more spontaneously. Wonderful. What will you do with them?

Your new challenge is to learn how to evaluate the quality of the *many* ideas you have. This means you need to become adept at deciding which ones are good ideas or even great ideas, storing those that need further study or have no immediate application, and setting the wheels in motion for effective idea implementation. We must look, then, at idea evaluation.

What's So Great About It?

Everybody knows what a great idea is. A great idea is the one that worked. Everybody can look at this great idea and say, "*What a Great Idea!*" Or they'll say, "Look at how simple *that* is!" Or, more likely, they'll say, "Why didn't *I* think of that?" Of course, they are correct in their assessment of greatness. They have the advantage of looking at an idea *after* someone evaluated it and determined that it was indeed a great idea, *after* someone nurtured it, *after* someone decided to run with it, *after* some people stuck their necks out, *after* the marketplace or organization or bosses or public opinion indeed got together, waved their hands in unison, and wildly agreed: "This is a great idea. We'll buy it!"

You, the lonely Idea Generator, however, don't have this advantage of 20/20 hindsight. You've just come up with an idea. Or someone else has come up with an idea. It sounds good. You like its approach, uniqueness, or other immediately apparent feature. But is the idea really good?

I want to give you some quick approaches to evaluation so that you can obtain an initial "feel" concerning an idea's relative merits. You can use this quick evaluation approach to gain a sense of your own perspective or to gather information from your organization or closest colleagues. Your overall objective, of course, is to pick winners, to choose ideas worthy of your time and resources.

Gut vs. Brain

As noted in the quotation at the beginning of this chapter, intuition discovers and the brain proves. But it is at the intuitive level that my evaluation system operates. We're not looking for the analytical evaluation, the numbers, the elaborate tests. They can all come later. What we're looking for in an initial, quick evaluation is the "gut reaction," yours, that of your closest colleagues, or perhaps even the gut reaction of the organization at large.

Thinkers and innovators have long known the importance of this initial, often visceral reaction. Einstein, for example, sensed that he was on the right track when he felt a tingling at the end of his fingers. A survey of top executives revealed other physical manifestations of the gut reaction:

1. *A growing excitement in the pit of my stomach.*

2. *A feeling of total harmony.*

3. *A total sense of commitment.*

4. *A burst of enthusiasm and energy.*

Sigmund Freud came up with a unique way to test out his gut feeling on a problem. He would flip a coin. First he would assign heads and tails to a yes/no decision. Then he'd flip. If the coin said yes and his gut said, "Let's go two out of three. I'm not comfortable with that decision!" then his intuitive reaction had just revealed itself.

Tuning In

You undoubtedly have your own set of feelings that you call your gut reaction. This intuition, this feeling, should serve as the very first evaluation you make of your ideas or of the direction you're heading in your search for ideas. To help you tune in to these reactions you already have, I've prepared a Great Idea Action Sheet on page 175 for you to complete. Doing so will aid you in describing what a "good idea" and a "bad idea" feel like.

> *Einstein felt a tingling in his fingertips; Freud watched his own reaction to the flip of a coin.*

Brain Check

Of course, evaluation is not just a touchy-feely process devoid of analytical thinking. Quite the contrary. Any evaluation necessarily depends on a mental process of isolating objectives (What do I want the idea to accomplish?), identifying the relevant criteria that determine the relative worth of an idea (What standards do I apply?), and allocating some sort of weight to those standards (How do I apply the standards?). Gathering this initial information requires analytical thinking. The best starting point, of course, is learning to ask the right questions.

Ask the Right Questions

In the creativity software IdeaFisher, you'll find thousands of questions enabling you to decipher and think about particular problems in need of creative solutions. I offer here several types of question that can help you begin the evaluation process. I've divided them into the following categories:

Failure

Success

Future

Personal

Mission

Timing

1. Ask about Failure

If you failed completely, what would happen?
If you failed partially, what would happen?
Are these risks and possible losses acceptable?
Can the risks and possible losses be avoided or reduced?
If you fail, what can you salvage?
If your idea is a product that fails, can you sell it as something else?
Should you throw everything out and start over?
What are the advantages and disadvantages of starting over?

2. Ask about Success

What criteria will you use to determine success?
Who is essential to the outcome?
What tangible thing is necessary?
What place or location is necessary?
What intangible or abstract thing is essential?
What action or process must happen?
What activity or event must occur?
What can you do to make your idea even better?
What can you get rid of without spoiling your success?

3. Ask about the Future

Will your idea be obsolete because of evolving technologies?
When will obsolescence occur?
How quickly and effectively can you respond?
If your idea is a product or service, what effect will it have on people's quality of life? Physical health? Mental health? Safety? Standards of living? Self-fulfillment?
How will your idea affect the quality of human and animal life fifty years from now?
If a patent is important, can you get one?
What is the longevity for your idea?
If the idea catches on suddenly, can you keep up with the demand?
Which of the following changed circumstances might affect your idea? How?

> Overseas competition
> Corporate takeover
> Change of management
> Availability of materials

Cost of materials
Fashion changes
Boycott
Political unrest
Societal change
Number of foreign visitors
Foreign investments in this country
Any others?

4. Ask Personal Questions

If it were *your* money, what would you do?
Are you changing merely for the sake of change? If so, is that wise?
How strong is your commitment to the project?
How strong is your desire to reach the goal?
How willing are you to invest the necessary time and energy?
Should you challenge any of your assumptions?
What are you taking for granted?
What are you assuming is impossible?
What do you assume are the givens?
What steps or procedures should you question?
What ideas should you question?
What facts should you question?
What if you were to ignore the problem? Would it solve itself?

5. Ask about Your Mission

Do you know exactly where this idea fits into the big picture?
Does it promote your mission?
Does it complement your other products and services?
Does it represent a step forward?
Have you been looking at this idea from all points of view or just
your own?

6. Ask about Timing

Is the idea timely?
Is it too late, at the end of a trend?
Is it too early, too much ahead of its time?
If it is too early, should you postpone your plans?

Beware of the Standard Evaluation Form

An evaluation form is a written or mental routine you go through when evaluating the quality of a new idea, suggestion, or procedure. Most evaluation forms ask for positives and negatives and force you to "weigh" these factors. Then you make some final tally and come up with a score, perhaps on a scale of one to ten, so that you can look at your idea and call it "an eight."

Some standard evaluation forms, with their emphasis on negatives, might force you to fling a host of Killer Phrases at yourself, killing off your idea before it has any chance of proving its worth. Also, the traditional forms tend to look at ideas from only two dimensions: goodness and badness, positives and negatives. The proverbial thumb points only up or down. Any "in-betweenness" shows up only in flat, or average, scores, say, a five on a scale of 1 to 10.

But in-betweenness might be the attractiveness or strength of an idea. This in-betweenness I like to call the "interest factor." For example,

> **CREATIVE RULE OF THUMB #17**
>
> **Often it's the interesting part of an idea—not the positive or negative— that leads to innovation.**

perhaps you think an idea is a bad one or a so-so one when evaluating it by your articulated standards. But maybe it has an "interesting" attribute. Maybe it's "appealing." An idea might have some positive attributes and some negative ones and still be extremely or even just moderately "interesting" or "intriguing." This attribute, this "interest factor," might prompt you to sit on the idea for a few days, to let it simmer, rather than dismiss it outright. This in-betweenness or interest factor might be the distinguishing characteristic of a truly great idea. Yet many evaluation forms ignore this potential.

To cure what I perceive to be a defect in traditional evaluation, I've devised a quick five-minute quality check you can use to help you form an initial reaction to an idea, whether your idea or that of someone else.

The Quick Five-Minute Quality Check

The initial evaluation should closely resemble the idea-generation process itself. The attempt should be to identify as many positive factors, as many negative factors, and as many interesting factors as you possibly can. Just listing these qualities will give you some notion of what your idea has going for it and against it. And forcing yourself to identify the *interesting* attributes of an idea can lead you to new ways of thinking about it, ways to refine it so that it does indeed mature into one of those great ideas we all seek.

The following chart, based on the Great Idea Action Sheet on page 176, can be printed on 4" x 6" note cards and filed in your Great Idea Box.

Describe the idea: File by: _____
                                                  Date: _____
                                                  Ranking: _____
                                                  Action Date: _____

Qualities of the idea:

Positive	Interesting	Negative
1. _____	1. _____	1. _____
2. _____	2. _____	2. _____
3. _____	3. _____	3. _____
4. _____	4. _____	4. _____
5. _____	5. _____	5. _____

(   ) X 2 = _____   + (   ) X 1 = _____   + (   ) X (-2) =   [   ]
                                                                    Total

The "Bull's-Eye"

After evaluating numerous ideas, how do you merge the efforts needed to take these ideas to completion into your busy schedule? Here's one way.

Break the idea down into doable weekly action chunks. Organizing on a weekly basis provides much greater balance and leeway for completion than the typical daily planning. In daily planning, crises always seem to take priority and push to do's from one day to the next.

I try to rank my daily activities by setting up a little tent card on my desk that portrays two sets of concentric circles:

In the right-hand circle, "nice to do" describes things that are important yet that have a low impact on my productivity or the outcomes I want to achieve. "Ought to do" items involve pressure from peers and society. "Must do" are the ones that deserve my attention even when my plate is overflowing with activities and responsibilities.

In the circle at the left, "concern" refers to things that concern me but that will not really change my situation, whereas "influence" heads up actions I can take that will have a direct influence on the outcome of my work. Naturally, I try to turn my attention away from the former and toward the latter.

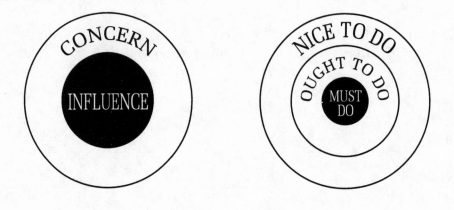

Reality Check

Evaluation and decision making are sciences in and of themselves. I don't pretend that this chapter has treated these complex processes in any significant degree of scientific detail. Yet evaluation relies on the gut and on the brain. The true innovators, indeed the true leaders, can feel inside whether or not they're on the right track. But these highly creative people also know how to use their conscious intellect and evaluate their ideas before committing time, money, and people to any given innovative scheme.

What Ideas Feel Like

Learn to recognize the qualities of your response to ideas by Idea Mapping both your positive and negative reactions.

Step 1 Idea Map your physical and mental reactions to ideas.

In the center of a blank sheet of paper place the Trigger Phrase, "Good one, go with it!" On another sheet of paper put "No, don't do it!" In five minutes, write down as many words as you can describing your mental and physical reactions to these gut messages. Work on both maps simultaneously as words occur to you. Draw arrows from one word to another connecting your key thoughts. Add more words as necessary.

Step 2 Look for the main concepts and patterns in your Idea Maps.

Assign geometric symbols to your main concepts and "cluster" your words by putting the respective symbol around each related word.

Step 3 Create an Idea Outline.

Now transcribe your Idea Maps into either "clusters" or a Roman-numeral outline.

Step 4 Record your feelings.

Write down four characteristics of your gut feeling that can help you in the process of evaluating new ideas.

"Good one, go with it!"   *"No, don't do it!"*

_____   _____

_____   _____

_____   _____

_____   _____

Five-Minute Quality Check

Write a brief description of the idea in the space provided. Review the list of "considerations" at the bottom of this page and add any further considerations relevant to your idea. Then identify and write down as many Positive Qualities, Negative Qualities, and Interesting Qualities as you can think of. Total the score by filling in the appropriate numbers.

Describe the idea:

Qualities of the idea:

Positive	Interesting	Negative
1.	1.	1.
2.	2.	2.
3.	3.	3.
4.	4.	4.
5.	5.	5.
6.	6.	6.
7.	7.	7.
8.	8.	8.
9.	9.	9.
10.	10.	10.

(   ) x 2 = _____   +   (   ) x 1 = _____   +   (   ) x (-2) = [   ]

Total

Considerations:

Cost savings, Improved performance, Improved service, Start-up cost, Measurable effectiveness, Public relations value, Distribution, Existing people/materials, Test marketability

Chapter 15

PUT IT WHERE YOU NEED IT
Managing and Retrieving Ideas

As you generate ideas, you need to find ways to manage them effectively. Ironically, many people don't know what to *do* with their ideas. I emphasize the word *do* because I want you to start thinking about ideas as *things*.

Most people unconsciously recognize this tangible nature of ideas. After all, what do you do when you get an idea? You write it down on a legal pad, or a napkin, or—in a real emergency—on the inside of your wrist. The idea becomes an object, an entity, a thing, a product.

And what do most people then *do* with their ideas? Stuff them in a hip pocket or purse. Drop them in a top drawer. Wash them off their wrist by mistake. Or the neat and organized types will "file them *away*." Most people, it's plain to see, don't treat their own great ideas with very much respect.

You indeed should begin to look at your ideas as *things*. As Dr. NakaMats discusses at the beginning of this book, there are even "invisible inventions"—"a new way of teaching something, a new way to spark creativity in others." Just think how empowered our teaching profession would feel if they realized that they were creating "invisible inventions" every time they developed a new curriculum or lesson plan.

> **CREATIVE RULE OF THUMB #18**
>
> **Writing down your ideas is like money in the bank.**

In fact, you should look at your ideas as *tangible assets*. Because they indeed are assets, you should treat them as such. You should develop, therefore, a system for storing and accessing your ideas.

The Great Idea Inventory Control System

You've got an idea. Or you've borrowed an idea. Or someone has brought an idea to your attention. You've given it a quality check. It "has a lot going for it." So what do you *do* with it?

Your objective, of course, is to implement the great ideas and to have bad ideas fail and fail fast. The entire decision-making process, of course, will take time. Also, many ideas might just be "little ideas," a quick brainstorm you have driving to work that you "must remember to look into when time permits." So while the wheels turn to decide on the big ideas or while you do other things and come up with even more big or little ideas, you need to keep track of all your ideas in some systematic way. You should have some method of recording your ideas, storing them, and retrieving them quickly and efficiently.

Think about your organization. You want to check your inventory of copy paper. You go to the supply closet, see the inventory is low, and order some more. Do you have a systematic way to check on the inventory of your ideas?

If you do, you're to be congratulated. If you don't, it's time to start a Great Idea Inventory Control System. When you have it up and running, then you'll be able to treat your ideas with respect, to review your inventory of ideas at any time, to retrieve an idea on any subject matter, to look after and pamper your mental assets.

File It *Away*?

Many people have an Idea File. In advertising, people call it a "Swipe File." In public relations, it's called a "Clip File." In these various files, people stuff little slips of paper, or interesting brochures, or interesting newspaper articles. They file ideas *away*. Ideas don't want to be filed *away*. To act as great ideas or potentially great ideas, they should be readily available, easily retrievable, and preferably *visible*.

Think about your own Idea File. When was the last time you put something in it? More important, when was the last time you took something *out* of it?

The bottom line, of course, is that your Idea File by itself isn't the best solution. Let's look at ways of improving your filing.

1. The Great Idea Book

Go to the store and buy a colorful notebook and some divider tabs. Divide your ideas into several different subject areas and open a tab for each one. The tabs, for example, in my own Great Idea Book read like this: "New Products," "New Services," "Workshop Materials," "Book Materials," "Promotional," "Distribution," and "Financial." Then, as you fill out your Control Sheets, put them into the correct index tab and alphabetize them by idea name or by keyword retrieval.

2. The Great Idea Recipe Box

If you're terse and can distill your ideas down to a phrase or two, then go to the store and buy a recipe box and a supply of index cards. Be sure to get some alphabetical dividers for easy retrieval. Then develop your own Great Idea Control Cards.

3. The Great Idea Rolodex

Rolodex Corporation will love this one. Put your ideas on Rolodex cards. Then you'll be able to flip to them with ease.

4. The Great Idea Computer System

Of course, all readers with personal computers will want to computerize their ideas. Using a data base system like Filemaker, HyperCard, Info Select, or Rapidfile, you should create a data base of ideas, which you could then search by word, number, dollar amount, date, or other field of information.

IdeaFisher, discussed in Chapter 4, allows you to add your own idea associations to its data base. The same is true of the program's QBank—you can add to its thousands of questions designed to help you define and transform your ideas.

You can even use word-processing packages to keep track of your ideas. Either open a new "document" for each Great Idea Control Sheet or have an "Idea Document" containing all your Control Sheets. Then you could use the index function to search your documents for a word pattern or the word-processing "search" function to search a single document containing all control sheets.

5. Frame It!

For your truly great ideas—those that you want to turn into goals or dreams—you should *frame them!* Find a photograph or a statement or draw a picture or write a line that expresses your idea or vision, frame it, and hang it prominently in your office or throughout your organization.

6. The Refrigerator Door

If you're lucky enough to have a refrigerator in your office or anywhere close by, go to the store and buy some of those magnetic refrigerator-door notice-holders. Then proceed to put your current ideas on your refrigerator door where they'll be constantly visible.

7. Freedom of Information

Ideally, in organizations, ideas belonging to any individual would be usable by any other individual. In the ideal world, you should be able to go to a central system or access a central computer system to find ideas developed by others. By having some central system, you could ensure that creativity would go up exponentially in your organization.

8. The Great Idea Control Sheet

To preserve your idea, you've got to commit it to paper or input it into your computer using words, numbers, or pictures. Forget the wrists and napkins. Instead, you should begin the habit of filling out a Control Sheet and systematically storing it for future use. To help you along, I've prepared a suggested Great Idea Control Sheet on the next page.

Retrieval as Inspiration

Because your ideas are your tangible products, and can lead to the betterment of your life and the lives of others, it only makes sense to treat them with the greatest respect. Thus you don't exile them to files or bins or cassettes that you'll only consult the next time you're cleaning out your office. You find ways to keep them in front of you, because they're guiding stars, in your own constellation.

Great Idea Control Sheet

Use a format like the following to record basic information about each of your ideas for future reference and retrieval.

Control #:_____   Keyword: _____

Idea Person: Telephone:

Idea Name:

Idea Description:

What impact will the idea have on:

1. Mission/Shared Vision:

2. Customer Satisfaction:

3. Service:

4. Speed:

5. Simplicity of Operations:

6. Employee Self-Confidence:

7. Morale:

8. Profit:

What successful ideas are similar:

1. _____

2. _____

3. _____

What areas need to be explored:

1. _____

2. _____

3. _____

What is going for it:

1. _____

2. _____

3. _____

What is going against it:

1. _____

2. _____

3. _____

Who are interested stakeholders:

1. _____

2. _____

3. _____

Do they have a different point of view?

1. _____

2. _____

3. _____

How we'll know if it's succeeding:

1. _____

2. _____

3. _____

How we'll know if it's failing:

1. _____

2. _____

3. _____

Chapter 16

SHOW BUSINESS
Idea Meetings That Work

Most of us have no real training in designing, participating in, or running an effective meeting. Yet we as a nation have more than eleven million meetings, and as a planet more than seventy million meetings every single workday. Ask yourself this question: "Have I ever held a meeting where little or nothing was accomplished?" Most of us would have to admit that we have held or certainly attended such meetings.

Most people take a rather dim view of meetings. If they are correct in their low evaluation of meetings (and I think they are), then I must conclude that most executives come up short in their ability to run a meeting. To paraphrase Peter Drucker, "We either work or we meet. We can't do both."

That's probably true for the vast majority of meetings held throughout the world. But I believe that with a little creative thinking, and the techniques we've learned in this book, we can make meetings work.

Meetings and Collaboration

Why do we have meetings?

Experts say that we should hold meetings for specific reasons, such as:

1. To give or exchange information.
2. To create or develop ideas.
3. To decide on goals or issues.
4. To delegate work or authority.
5. To share work or responsibility.
6. To persuade, involve, or inspire.
7. To establish or maintain relations.

Each of these reasons to hold a meeting has its own set of dynamics, its own requirement for success, and its own mix of participants. To be successful, experts say that you should never mix a "develop new ideas" meeting with a "share your work" meeting. Instead, you should call two meetings.

This approach might have been a great idea in the MBO (Management by Objective) 1980s. Indeed, it probably accounts for the reported national 38 percent increase in daily meetings from 1987 to 1989.

The approach has serious drawbacks in the 1990s, which will be characterized by a "boundaryless" mind-set that continually looks for synergy. One of the best ways to find that synergy, according to Schrage, in *Shared Minds*, is by encouraging true collaboration. Changing our focus from individual performance to group creation, Schrage suggests, will transform our ideas about meetings and how they can work.

According to Schrage, we've been using the technologies of communication—everything from pens and paper to overhead projectors to faxes to the latest computer and video setups—to transmit individual experiences rather than create something in common. Traditional meetings and other attempts at communication frustrate people partly because they're examples of individuals forwarding their own ideas or agendas, and other individuals reacting, all too often with boredom or cynicism. But true collaboration, Schrage says, is not just the sum of individual actions; it's the generation of "shared understandings" that the individuals "couldn't possibly have achieved on their own."

> *Meetings can play an important part in changing our focus from individual performance to group creation.*

As explained by John Dykstra, leader of the special-effects team for the *Star Wars* films, ordinary communication is trying "to tell someone something you know"; in collaboration, "you're both trying to create something you *don't* know."

"So you try to get a communal mind going; you want to get people's minds to interact as components of a larger mind—one person's logical sense, one person's visual sense, another person's acoustic sense. You get a communal brain. What matters is not just the individual talents but the ability to integrate them" (Schrage, *Shared Minds*).

Schrage noted that the word *collaboration* is missing entirely from the indexes of the most popular books on management, including all of those by Peter Drucker, *In Search of Excellence*, and *The One-Minute Manager*. The emphasis instead is on "communication," yet most organizations are not able to use communication skills to create a genuine spirit of companywide creativity.

The most exciting example Schrage (*Shared Minds*) gave of how collaboration can change meetings is the "Colab" format used at Xerox Corporation's Palo Alto Research Center. There each participant has a personal computer with which to send information to a large screen at the front of the room.

> *To promote shared viewing and access, Colab is built around a team interface concept known as WYSIWIS (pronounced "whizzy whiz") for "what you see is what I see." The Colab software lets participants partition the large screen into multiple windows . . . that can be enlarged, shrunk, thrown away, moved around, linked, clustered, or stored for later retrieval. Participants can also "telepoint" to windows and objects on the screen to identify subjects of interest or topics of concern.*

Unlike the words in an oral exchange, everything placed on the screen—including graphics and symbols—can be kept in front of the group for consideration and for revision, and then can be printed out at the end. In an interesting parallel to Idea Mapping, Xerox also uses a software that can generate an annotated outline of the session.

You might not have a giant computer setup and cutting-edge software, yet Idea Mapping in meetings is one step you can take now to encourage a genuine collaborative spirit. Of the traditional situation Schrage says, "What we have here is a linear montage of speeches, soliloquies, conversations, arguments, interjections, visual displays, gestures, and grunts all presented within a certain time frame within the same room. It's called a meeting."

"The key," he believes, "is to create an environment that shifts attention away from the individual participant and toward community expression." In the case of Xerox at Palo Alto, the focus is on a computer screen, but moving the focus to an Idea Map or other graphic display, as long as it's being created by the group, is a way to begin achieving the same kind of result.

Mapping the Meeting

Let's reframe our concept of a meeting by creating a simile.

A meeting is like . . . a performance.

Our Idea Map on the next page with "successful performance" as the Trigger Word yields the following elements:

great script	*no stand-ins*
specified times for acts	*audience*
experienced actors	*no heckling*
starting air time	*cue cards*
director	*applause*
intermission	*lights*
warm-up	*program*
props	*scheduling*

The Basics

1. Great Script

A great script that both actors and director follow is analogous to a written meeting agenda received at least two days before the meeting. I always use Idea Mapping to generate my initial agenda items and then transcribe them in a linear outline for distribution. I've also found that putting the amount of time allocated next to each agenda item serves the same function as breaking a play into Act I, Act II, and so on.

2. Scheduling

Timing can be crucial to the success of a meeting. According to a survey by Accountemps, Inc., Tuesday is the day when people are most productive and motivated to learn. When asked "What is the best day for holding a training program?" personnel directors responded:

Tuesday	*59%*
Wednesday	*9%*
Thursday	*6%*
Friday	*2%*
Monday	*0%*

The rest thought that the day of the week made no difference.

3. Warm-Up

In a rock concert or a standup comic show, preliminary bands or lesser-known comedians will warm up the crowd before the main attraction performs. How can we warm up our meeting participants? The best way I know is to bring in a prop, which can be a simple box of baking soda or a box of Crayola crayons. Challenge your group to come up with thirty uses for the baking soda or crayons. The record for baking soda in my creativity workshops was set as this book went to press. A group of Hewlett-Packard dealer salespeople came up with eighty-three uses of baking soda in three minutes flat. (In honor of the record, the names of the participants are listed in the appendix.) You'll find that warming up your crowd will pay handsome dividends throughout the rest of the meeting. To get you started with the all-important warm-up exercises, I've prepared some Great Idea Action Sheets, which you'll find at the end of this chapter.

> **CREATIVE RULE OF THUMB #19**
>
> **Always start a sixty-minute meeting with a one-minute warm-up exercise.**

4. Props

My favorite props are a box of Crayola crayons and a stack of unruled paper. Let your participants Idea Map with the crayons; watch the child come out as they're sharing the colors. You can also use the paper for Killer Phrase-fighting paper wads.

5. No Stand-Ins

Nothing's worse than showing up for a play only to find that the lead actor has been replaced by an understudy. Great meetings start *on time* with all participants present and ready.

6. Cue Cards

The notion of "cue cards" triggers for me the idea of writing key issues on flip charts or marker boards, or on large poster boards on the walls of the meeting room.

7. No Heckling

Killer Phrases aren't allowed. Levy fines or punish offenders with hurled paper wads. I also recommend putting up a list of potential Killer Phrases.

8. Applause

Audiences like to give feedback. Use large marker boards or put "butcher paper" on one wall and have your meeting members Idea Map their problems right there in the meeting. Provide plenty of colorful markers, preferably the nontoxic ones that smell like various types of fruit.

9. Intermission

We all know how important a well-placed intermission is. Remember the three B's: brain, bladder, and butt. Each can only go sixty to ninety minutes without a break.

A Command Performance—Brainstorming Meetings

I think the best environment for brainstorming is in a meeting. Great Idea Meetings are best scheduled for first thing in the morning, preferably not following lunch and, please, *never* after dinner.

Another important point: To make certain that you achieve a "no holds barred except fouls" brainstorming dialogue, the boss or team leader should not run this part of the meeting. Instead, rotate this responsibility among the staff. Otherwise, the boss might be dangerously inclined to squelch the views of others. The only views that ought to be squelched are personal verbal attacks. Thus the atmosphere should be "no holds barred *except fouls.*"

This Great Idea Meeting is more like improvisational theater, so you need someone with quick and legible writing to act as an Idea Recorder. It's usually best to use Idea Maps on large flip charts, marker boards, or butcher paper taped to the walls.

When the Curtain Goes Up

At the beginning of the meeting, you need to orient participants with a short introduction that covers the following:

1. *The goals of the meeting.*

2. *The agenda.*

3. *If it's a problem-solving meeting:*

    a. *The problem and its history.*

    b. *Its likely consequences if not solved.*

    c. *The benefits when the problem is solved.*

4. *The appointment of the Idea Recorder and the Brainstorm Facilitator.*

The Cast of Characters

If you want to institutionalize the Great Idea Meeting in your organization, you might want to consider creating an Innovation Team. Large organizations are beginning to see the advantages of the small-team approach to idea making. They had to, when statistics showed that more than two-thirds of all inventions were created by individuals on their own time or by small organizations. That was indeed hard data to

> *Two-thirds of all inventions are created by individuals on their own time or by small organizations.*

swallow when the big organizations realized that they were spending roughly 85 percent of all research-and-development money.

The challenge for the large organization is to set up small, focused innovation teams to meet specific, recognized needs. Although it might sound simple— Quick: appoint a team!—we are seldom taught how to form such a team or how to make it function as a group.

In staffing such a team, recall that creativity as a process involves different types of people. As noted in Chapter 1, from the beginning of an idea to its ultimate fruition, people with varying abilities and traits must play vital roles: the Idea Generator, the Idea Promoter, the Idea Systems Designer, the Idea Implementer, the Idea Evaluator.

Although you can assign these roles to members of the Innovation Team, it's often effective to try to find people who exhibit these traits to begin with, appoint them to the team, provide them the necessary wherewithal and support, and watch them work. The traits they might exhibit look like this:

The Idea Generators

They are typically the people whose main focus is on ideas themselves, not on organizational advancement or status. Their main drive in life is to deal with ideas and concepts. Sometimes Idea Generators are individuals who choose not to develop other skills, including social skills, because their focus is so overwhelmingly on concepts and ideas. Their strengths include primarily their brilliance, insights, dedication, and consuming passion for discovery. These are the inventors, the tinkerers, the discoverers. You'll find them all over the place. They populate R&D departments, product development, government research labs, government departments of policy analysis and research, and the faculties of colleges and universities throughout the world.

The Idea Promoters

The Idea Promoters often take the idea of the Idea Generator, recognize its application and potential, and begin to put the wheels in motion for implementation. On the up side, the Idea Promoters are enthusiastic, resourceful, charismatic, and positive. They refuse to succumb to defeat. If something doesn't work, they'll try something else. They willingly take risks, whether it's the risk of their own or someone else's fortunes. At the end of the line, they always picture success, a world where all their predictions come true. On the down side, the Idea Promoters can be so single-minded that they fail to recognize reality. Often they won't listen to an opposing, negative view and won't hesitate to break institutional rules in pursuit of their dreams. Their enthusiasm can be overwhelming and often exhausting to other people.

The Idea Designers

Idea Designers, who get the idea from the Idea Generator and its application and vision from the Idea Promoter, can then see how to assemble the financial, manpower, manufacturing, or other systems necessary to make the idea work. These are the planners and designers—the ones who can picture what's needed to accomplish a desired end. They can paint the broad strokes. They can picture what the organizational chart should look like. They can predict and plan each step needed along the way toward realization of the idea.

The Idea Implementers

The Idea Implementers relish making things work according to the design set up by the Idea Designer. They would rather "go by the book" than question the way things are. They want to know what the rules are, what the policy is, what the required procedures are. Given those rules, policies, and procedures, they will meticulously follow all necessary steps toward the idea's realization. The downside, of course, is that they can be so focused on established procedures that they emphasize only limits and obstacles, in effect offering up Killer Phrases based on the routine. When attuned to a new idea, however, they become the greatest allies of its success.

Idea evaluators have an opinion about everything. They're supposed to.

The Idea Evaluators

The Idea Evaluators have an opinion about everything. They're supposed to. That's what they do. They look at the way things work or don't work and reach an unshakable opinion about why they work or don't work. They have their standards, whether dictated to them by the organization or created by them according to their own opinions. Whatever the source of these standards, they will apply them uniformly and consistently. They rarely accept things the way they are, always assuming that a flaw is just around the corner waiting for their discerning eye. This works both for and against the new idea, depending on whether the Idea Evaluator is just negative and critical, or simply ruthless and inquisitive. Of course, by applying techniques for diffusing Killer Phrases and for selling within the organization, you can convert an Idea Evaluator who seems negative into one who exercises clarity and fairness.

Once these Idea People are assembled or identified, they should then be *appointed* to serve on the Innovation Team or encouraged to *volunteer* for membership on the team. The policies and procedures guiding their respective duties and efforts might look like this:

Appointed Team	**Voluntary Team**
Given issues	*Self-generated issues*
Meets during work hours	*Meets after hours*
Four to seven participants	*Four to seven participants*
Elects responsibilities	*Elects responsibilities*
Staff assistance	*No staff assistance*
Reports every three months	*Reports every three months or sooner*
Needs to know funding limits	*Needs to know funding limits*
Six- to twelve-month commitment	*Commitment determined by team*

When the Innovation Team meets, it should follow the procedures already discussed for holding successful Great Idea Meetings. As it begins to work its magic, it can keep score to see whether its performance will receive the sought-after "rave reviews." A suggested "scorecard" follows in the next Great Idea Action Sheet.

Innovation Team Scorecard

Check the actions or attitudes of the following members of an Innovation Team.

Idea Generator

☐ Generated a lot of ideas.
☐ Sought out new alternatives, new responses, new ways.
☐ Stressed achieving results over conforming to rules and procedures.
☐ Focused almost solely on ideas and concepts.
☐ Asked, "What if . . . ," not "Here's why we can't . . ."

Idea Promoter

☐ Visualized the end result.
☐ Maintained optimism.
☐ Saw potential applications and impacts of new programs.
☐ Refused to allow setbacks to derail enthusiasm.
☐ Communicated team purpose in a way that provides momentum.
☐ Promoted ideas to organization.

Idea Designer

☐ Encouraged atmosphere of openness.
☐ Buffered team from outside limiting forces.
☐ Saw the big picture to identify resources needed to complete project.
☐ Created step-by-step procedures necessary for success.
☐ Defined performance standards.
☐ Provided structure and guidance.

Idea Implementer

☐ Saw to the details needed for overall team success.
☐ Filled in the blanks left by the Generator and Promoter.
☐ Played by the book.

Idea Evaluator

☐ Displayed concern when deadlines missed or policies ignored.
☐ Provided feedback on team performance.
☐ Made clear-cut decisions when required.
☐ Ensured that resources were applied productively.
☐ Ensured that projects were guided by clear plans and budgets.
☐ Insisted that performance standards were maintained.

Systems for Group Decisions

A powerful tool for generating creative collaboration in meetings is "group decision support systems." This is software, some of it approaching the complexity of Xerox's Colab, which allows participants to register their reactions to ideas and proposals into a shared computer via individual keypads. Michael Finley, writing in *IABC Communication World* ("The New Meaning of Meetings," March 1991), echoes Schrage's description of the traditional meeting as a rather simple,

> *"Meetings used to be such simple things." Now group decision support systems help make meetings far more complex—and richly productive.*

linear, individualistic affair. "Meetings used to be such simple things," Finley notes. "You told people to show up, they brought pencils and yellow pads. You told them what was on your mind, they told you what was on theirs." Group decision support systems (GDSS) can transform this scenario radically.

Of course, we all know that the constraints, limitations—and tensions—of the conventional meeting often mean that participants *don't* really get a chance, or feel free, to "tell you what's on their minds." An interesting aspect of electronic meetings is that they tend to encourage participation by those who might ordinarily shy away from it. A "mysterious attribute" of some of the systems, says Schrage, is that they can also encourage people "to think beyond the usual cramped confines of what they think is permitted."

The simplest GDSS packages are not much more than "voting" devices—keypads that allow participants to register yes and no responses; the more complex are more interactive, and allow participants to respond to, and evaluate, questions and ideas presented in a variety of media. The smallest programs involve people with individual keypads gathering around a single PC; the largest create multimedia electronic meeting rooms.

Robert Bostrom, of the University of Georgia's College of Business Administration, notes an interesting link between GDSS and the idea of changing perspectives to gain a more creative mind-set. As quoted by Finley, Bostrom says that "GDSS software has the capability to get you to step outside yourself and into someone else's shoes." Linked immediately to the responses of all the other participants, as the others are linked to yours, and freed from many of the social pressures of the meeting, you become "uncluttered by your own mind-set and concerns" and "free to do some truly creative problem solving, as a group." A result, even when participants are getting little more than immediate yes and no tallies from the group, can be a kind of group thinking.

As in any other field of communication, GDSS can be vulnerable to the effects of Killer Phrases. Those who are computer shy will need to overcome the internalized idea that they can't participate. Killer Phrases might be also hurled by managers who want to hold on to the old, more controlled style of meeting—for example, "We don't want some computer making our decisions for us." But, as Finley points out, "The best programs are discreet. They don't decide, they don't intrude. They simply guide you through the process."

And yet the GDSS process could conceivably encourage its own Killer Phrases, linked to a "group think" mentality in the negative sense. It remains to be seen whether GDSS enthusiasts will ever resort to Killer Phrases to discourage an iconoclast who wants to work outside that system.

I've provided a listing of GDSS software packages and suppliers in the Resources section.

When the Curtain Goes Down

On the following Great Idea Action Sheets, I've provided a variety of exercises to help you get warmed up and loosened up creatively in your next Great Idea Meeting. At the end of the meeting, whether of your Innovation Team or of your office staff, you should make sure that you answer two key questions:

"What now?" and

"Who needs to do what?"

Every meeting must inspire the group to commit to the task at hand. The participants must know what they need to do as a group and as individuals. They should get some notion that something worthwhile has been accomplished. They should get a feeling of "The End." At least for now.

Otherwise you'll just have to call another meeting to find out why the first one didn't work.

The Baking Soda Warm-Up

Take three minutes to write down as many uses as you can for baking soda. Let your mind blast away in divergent directions. Be bizarre! The most outrageous use for baking soda gets a free box. The record is eighty-three different uses.

1.	31.
2.	32.
3.	33.
4.	34.
5.	35.
6.	36.
7.	37.
8.	38.
9.	39.
10.	40.
11.	41.
12.	42.
13.	43.
14.	44.
15.	45.
16.	46.
17.	47.
18.	48.
19.	49.
20.	50.
21.	51.
22.	52.
23.	53.
24.	54.
25.	55.
26.	56.
27.	57.
28.	58.
29.	59.
30.	60.

Life of a Bookworm Exercise

This exercise challenges your problem-solving style. Are you analytical, spatial, or can you apply both modes when necessary?

Each of the four volumes depicted below has the same number of pages and the width from the first to the last page of each volume is two inches. Each volume has two covers and each cover is one-sixth of an inch thick.

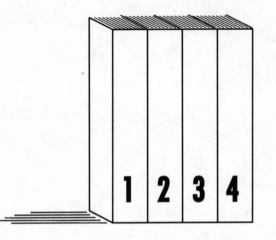

Our microscopic bookworm was born on page one of volume one. During his life he ate a straight hole across the bottom of the volumes. He ate all the way to the last page of volume four. The bookworm ate in a straight line, without zigzagging. The volumes are in English and are right-side up on a bookcase shelf.

Challenge: How many inches did the bookworm travel during his life?

Your Answer: _____

The Nine Dots Revisited

This exercise challenges your assumptions about the problem you are trying to solve. Are you willing to let go of your assumptions to find the solution?

Challenge: Connect these nine dots with four straight lines. (Once you start drawing the first line you cannot lift your writing utensil off the paper. You can cross over another line, but you cannot retrace the same line.)

Now try it with two straight lines.   **Finally, try it with only one line.**

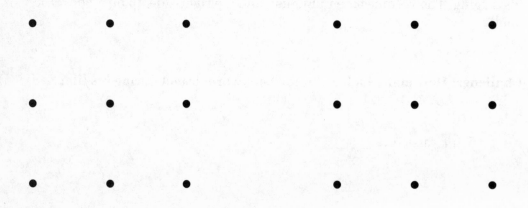

Making the Strange Familiar

Acts of creativity usually can be reduced to small, common steps of discovery.
Many of these involve turning seemingly unrelated, strange occurrences into flashes
of discovery.

Challenge: Decode the following groups of words and lines into common
phrases. For example, the translation of number 1 is "thermal underwear."

Wear	me quit
thermal	
0	knee
B.S.	light
M.A.	
Ph.D.	
r/e/a/d/i/n/g	ecnalg
t	w
o	o
u	r
c	h
h	t
moth	i i i
cry	O O
cry	

Please answer the following questions:

Did you feel a sense of discovery?

If you saw this grouping again, would you also see the common phrase?

Did recognizing a pattern help you decode?

The Power of a Killer Phrase

This exercise shows the power of the Killer Phrase and the need for challenging it in everyday activities.

The historic conquest of North America progressed from east to west following the New World's discovery in 1492. What if Columbus had given in to the Killer Phrase of the day—"Everyone knows the earth is flat"—and never set sail? Then, what if years later a courageous explorer had discovered the New World on the west coast, thus leading to settlement from west to east?

Challenge: How would the United States be different in language, politics, religion, wars, food, sports, and holidays?

1. Language:

2. Politics:

3. Religion:

4. Wars:

5. Food:

6. Sports:

7. Holidays:

How would you have diffused the Killer Phrase "Everybody knows the earth is flat"? What other Killer Phrases common in Columbus's time have courageous individuals and organizations overcome?

What a Great Idea! Copyright © 1992 by Charles "Chic" Thompson.

The Second Right Answer

This exercise demonstrates the benefits of revisiting your challenges and looking for additional answers.

Challenge: Count the number of squares you see in the design below.

1st Answer _____

Now, look for some more.

2nd Answer _____

Now, look for still more.

3rd Answer _____

The need for second right answers is summed up by philosopher Emile Chartier:

"Nothing is more dangerous than an idea when it's the only one you have."

Write down on another sheet of paper a time when a "second right answer" provided the solution you needed. Then list three challenges where you currently have solutions that could be revisited to find a second right answer.

What a Great Idea! Copyright © 1992 by Charles "Chic" Thompson.

Answers to Action Sheet Exercises

Answer to Life of a Bookworm Exercise:

If you said nine inches, you attempted to solve this problem with a straight numerical approach. To get the correct answer you need to think first from a spatial point of view. The correct answer is five inches, because the first page of each book is on the right side of the volume. The last page is on the left side. Pull out four books, put them on a shelf, pretend you're the worm, and see that, indeed, your trip covers just five inches.

Three solutions to the Nine Dots Revisited:

Assumption	**Challenge Action**
With four lines:	
Keep lines inside of box formed by dots.	Allow lines to go outside of the box.
With two lines:	
Use a standard pencil.	Use a wide marker that touches two dots.
With one line:	
Keep paper flat.	Accordion-fold paper between dots.

Answers to Making the Strange Familiar:

Top to bottom: thermal underwear; three degrees below zero; reading between the lines; touchdown; mothballs; quit following me; neon light; backwards glance; throw up; circles under the eyes.

Answers to the Second Right Answer:

At first sixteen individual squares; then one square surrounding the sixteen; then nine squares made up of four small squares; and finally, four squares of nine small squares. Total is thirty for a two-dimensional graphic.

CONCLUSION

Even though it may appear to involve a blizzard of details and analysis—and certainly control sheets, quality checks, and force fields strengthen that impression—the phase of *action* is a product of creativity and a field for the application of great ideas, just like every other step we've covered.

In our world, creativity isn't fully creative until we bring it into physical reality. As we saw in the third step, *creation*, your ideas won't make it into reality unless you see reality as something you can change. In *action*, the aspect of reality that you're altering is simply different. Here creativity works on communication with the other people and organizations whose help you need to make ideas real. *Action* also involves a creative approach to your own internal order of communication and organization—your ways of evaluating, accessing, and using your ideas.

Having recreated reality by formulating ideas, we need to reorganize reality in order to make ideas work. This means we must do much more than simply exercise creativity in our own minds. We must see creativity as something we bring to our meeting with other minds. We may need to allow that the most satisfying *action* of all could be the experience of working anew, with others, in creative concert.

Chapter 17

WHERE YOU LIVE
The Home of Creativity

As Yoshiro NakaMats suggests at the beginning of this book, creativity is no longer only 1 percent inspiration, 99 percent perspiration. Inspiration is now the critical creative force. Truly creative people receive inspiration from all facets of their lives—their work, their thoughts, their play, their family, their friends, their home. Thus the creative process doesn't start and stop. It continues as an ongoing process.

If you don't already, you should take creativity home with you. You can encourage a creative outlook in every member of your family and especially you can begin at once to diffuse that Killer Phrase "I'm not creative" you often hear from those you love.

Might I suggest a four-part process to spark your creativity at home?

Part One: The Dinner Table

Listen to your family's dinner conversation, including your own, and see if you recognize any Killer Phrases or other stifling actions. Then ask everyone when and where they tend to have their best ideas and most significant feelings. Ask if they bounce these ideas off other members of the family. You'll probably find that we don't make ample time for listening to the ideas of others, especially children and teenagers.

See if you can establish that from now on dinner time will be a "safe" place for new ideas, a time when anyone can bring up ideas that come into their minds. Then tell everyone what Killer Phrases are. Confess to those you know *you* use at home. Ask if there are any others your family has heard you say. Be prepared. You'll be surprised at the number of Killer Phrases you yourself use at home!

> *You can make your family dinner table a safe place for new ideas . . . but look out for your own Killer Phrases!*

On another evening, after the dishes are cleared, pull out a large piece of white paper and show your family what Idea Mapping is all about. Start off by putting the word *weekend* in the center and give everyone a pencil, pen, or crayon, and have them write down keywords describing what they want to do that weekend.

After a few minutes, have everyone step back to see the big picture. Have one person draw arrows connecting similar ideas about new, more creative weekend activities. Another evening, do the same thing with *vacation*. Or before a child's birthday, have him or her Idea Map the ideal gift.

After mapping the ideal gift, teach your family my favorite creativity technique: the power of opposite thinking. Have them Idea Map "What I would never want for my birthday." Then compare the maps and see if you can turn an opposite into a never-thought-of great idea.

Then, down the line, you can show your children how to use opposite thinking, metaphorical thinking, assumption challenging, and all the other creativity devices we've used in this book. Show them how many of these mental approaches can and do apply directly to their schoolwork. Have your child use an Idea Map as a preliminary outline for a book report or theme.

Part Two: Go to Your Room

Remember when "Go to your room" was the ultimate Killer Phrase, the ultimate punishment? These days, with many teenagers' rooms equipped with stereo, computer, TV, and a host of other high-tech gear, "Go to your room" should become an invitation to creativity.

Along with the inevitable high-tech equipment, a teenager's room should be equipped with a large marker board or butcher paper on the walls. Encourage your children to use Idea Mapping for their homework assignments. You'll be amazed how much easier it will be to remember the causes of the Civil War if you Idea Map them with your children. Then leave the Idea Map on the wall until test time and watch their grades improve. A roll of butcher paper works great on the wall, because you can roll it up and refer to it later.

Many educators are now advocating background music during

study time. Not hard rock, or rap. But largo classical movements, those with beats slower than the normal heartbeat. As mentioned earlier, such music has been found to produce a sense of balance and to improve concentration. A few recommended classical selections are listed on page 147 at the end of Chapter 12.

Part Three: The Bedroom

If you think this section is about creative bedroom activities, you're right. Sex has been shown to increase creativity, by providing a break mentally and physically. Interestingly, abstinence also increases creativity, by providing and allowing a focused concentration. But other things happen in the bedroom. Sleep. And dreams.

A great deal of research has been done on the relationship between dreaming and creativity. A dream is our moment of pure creativity. It's like five hundred ideas all Scotch-taped together. In your dreams, which normally comprise 20 percent of your sleep time, you are the producer, the director, the actor, the cast of characters, and the cameraperson in your own epic.

Noteworthy Dreamers

Throughout our history, great thinkers have used and relied on their dreams as guides to the creative process. We've mentioned Friedrich von Kekule, the chemistry professor who in 1890 dreamed the solution to the structure of the benzene molecule and revolutionized organic chemistry. There have, of course, been many others.

In the 1850s, Elias Howe couldn't get his newly developed lock-stitch sewing machine to work properly. In a nightmare of being boiled alive, he noticed that the cannibals' spears all had holes in the tips. Howe awoke with the idea of threading a needle at the tip rather than at the middle, like conventional sewing machine needles.

General George Patton's personal secretary was frequently called on in the middle of the night to take dictation after Patton had been startled awake with a fully formed battle plan.

Much more recently, Alan Huang, now the head of AT&T Bell Laboratories' Optical Computing Research Department, used a recurring dream to make what *Success* magazine called "the greatest breakthrough in computer science since the microchip." Huang's dream was that two opposing armies of sorcerer's apprentices carried pails of data toward each other but stopped short of colliding. Then, one night, the armies passed through each other. To Huang, they were like "light passing through light."

For years Huang had been trying to solve the problem of creating an optical computer, using laser beams. The dream told him that because laser beams would pass through each other, unlike electric currents, they each didn't need their own pathways. "Then I knew," Huang says, "there was a way." And he has since proven that lasers can function as a new type of computer.

Huang's message is to listen to the unconscious. "Too often," he says, "we are shamed into not going with our instincts." An inventor, he says, must be willing to look foolish; unique ideas can be lost through self-censorship: "Oh, that's ridiculous" or "It's just a dream" or "No one will understand." I think I understand Huang, because, for one thing, he's always been hampered by dyslexia and so never felt comfortable with words and equations. But, "early in childhood, he 'saw' mathematical equations as having shapes and colors" (Jason Forsythe, "The Dream Machine," *Success*, October 1990).

Perhaps someday a popular question will be: What color is your equation?

Recording Your "Dreamed-Up" Ideas

I have found it very beneficial to learn how to record my dreams. For the record, we all dream and we all dream in color. If you are now saying the Killer Phrase "I never dream" or "I can't remember my dreams," allow your mind to be open and read on.

Here are some steps to successfully remember, record, and interpret your dreams.

1. *As you are falling asleep, state that you want to remember your dreams.*
2. *On awakening, do not open your eyes for at least one minute. Think back to any dreams that you had and play them back in your mind.*
3. *Record the dream immediately on paper using an Idea Map and look for any metaphors that may symbolize a real-life problem.*
4. *Give the dream a title and file it for further reference.*

Tomorrow Morning's Assignment

Use an Idea Map to explore one dream that you've had. If you can't remember one, try again tonight.

Record Your Semiconscious Ideas

Just as you are falling asleep and just as you are waking up are key times of free association. One music historian observed that Bach did most of his composing while lying in bed after a nap. (Reputedly, he also had nineteen children!)

Keep a pad of paper and a pen in front of your alarm clock so that the display provides some light. Be prepared to write down ideas or images you have right before falling asleep or immediately on waking up. Do not be discouraged if some of your thoughts do not make any sense. Remember, you're after large quantities of ideas. Just throw the bad ones away.

Part Four: The Bathroom

Remember the top ten idea-friendly times. Number 1 and Number 2 occur in the bathroom. Here they are again:

   10. While performing manual labor.

   9. While listening to a church sermon.

   8. After waking up in the middle of the night.

   7. While exercising.

   6. While reading.

   5. During a boring meeting.

   4. While falling asleep or waking up.

   3. While commuting to work.

   2. While showering or shaving.

   1. While sitting on the toilet!

The Greek scientist Archimedes was taking a bath when he realized that water displacement could be used to determine the

> ### CREATIVE RULE OF THUMB #20
>
> **Make friends with your shower. If inspired to sing, maybe the song has an idea in it for you.**
> **—Albert Einstein**

composition of different metals in the king's crown. Ecstatic and quite naked, he ran to tell the king, shouting "Eureka, Eureka!" If only Archimedes had had a pad of our Great Idea Notes, he might have saved himself considerable embarrassment.

So along with the *Readers Digest* and an adequate supply of Charmin, keep pads of paper and pens at hand in the bathroom. Right there in the middle of a shave, a brush, or a flush, you might find great ideas.

No End, No Limit

Some people think that our civilization is in decline, that we've lost our spark, and that culture as we know it is receding. I believe that what these observers are seeing is merely the evidence of profound, powerful change—change that demonstrates our growth and vitality. The most fundamental change I see occurring is the breaking down of barriers to the human spirit.

The creative human spirit has given notice that it cannot and will not be contained. Now we live in a time when it *must* be free, in order for us to find a way to live in harmony with our home, the earth. Because necessity is the mother of invention, and the necessity for change is so compelling, you can be sure that we're in store for great innovations. And we can see everywhere that the human mind and spirit is rising to the task.

The spark that sustains our creativity could simply be called love, for I believe that the great thinkers, inventors, and artists of this world are really those who love life and who feel free to give to it what they receive from it. In order for that spark to burn, we need to be free, within and without, as Yoshiro NakaMats said at the beginning of this book. That's the precondition for creativity—and that's the wave we now see moving over our planet:

Freedom. What a great idea.

Afterword

"So how creative am I?"

You might ask yourself the above question. Or you might not, having surmised by now that creativity isn't a quantity, or a prize, or a point, but a state of being, in continual motion—a process.

The best measure of creativity is your enjoyment of the flow state of ideas. This is the source—the source of satisfaction for the innovator, the source of excellent results on behalf of consumers, clients, and organizations.

We have seen many organizational programs come and go: T Groups, Sensitivity Training, Quality Circles, Theory X, then Y, then Z Management. But increasing the creativity of people in organizations is one "program" that won't go away. For only those who are free to innovate will flourish.

Creativity can be called a mind-set, the current term for "frame of mind." It's a way of doing things. Most of all, and in every sense, it's a way of life.

Suggested Further Reading

Adams, James L. *The Care and Feeding of Our Ideas: A Guide to Encouraging Creativity.* Reading, Mass: Addison-Wesley Publishing Co., 1986.

Agor, Weston H., ed. *Intuition in Organizations: Leading and Managing Productively.* Newbury Park: Sage Publications, 1989.

Ahlbach, John. "Juggling and What It Can Do for You." San Francisco: National Stuttering Project, n.d.

Anakar, Paul. "Thinking Tools: The Next Computer Movement!" in *The Mindware Catalog.* Santa Cruz, Calif: The Mindware Review, 1991.

Anderson, Duncan Maxwell. "Seize the Future Now!" *Success,* October 1990.

Briggs, John. *Fire in the Crucible: The Alchemy of Creative Genius.* New York: St. Martin's Press, 1988.

Buzan, Tony. *Use Both Sides of Your Brain.* Rev. ed. New York: E. P. Dutton, 1983.

Cappachione, Lucia. *The Power of Your Other Hand: A Course in Channeling the Inner Wisdom of the Right Brain.* North Hollywood, Calif.: Newcastle Publishing Co., 1988.

Cassidy, John and B. C. Rimbeaux. *Juggling for the Complete Klutz.* Stanford, Calif.: Klutz Press, 1977.

Csikszentmihalyi, Mihaly. *Flow: The Psychology of Optimal Experience. Steps Toward Enhancing the Quality of Life.* New York: Harper & Row, 1990.

Feingold, S. Norman. *Futuristic Exercises: A Workbook on Emerging Lifestyles and Careers in the 21st Century and Beyond.* Garrett Park, Md.: Garrett Park Press, 1989.

Finley, Michael. "The New Meaning of Meetings," *IABC Communication World,* March 1991.

Forsythe, Jason. "The Dream Machine," *Success,* October 1990.

Geber, Beverly. "Speed: Where the People Fit In," *Training,* August 1989.

Gleick, James. *Chaos: Making a New Science.* New York: Viking-Penguin, 1987.

Goodspeed, Bennett W. *The Tao Jones Average: A Guide to Whole-Brained Investing.* New York: Penguin Books, 1983.

Hakuta, Ken. *How to Create Your Own Fad and Make a Million Dollars.* New York: William Morrow, 1988.

Handy, Charles. *The Age of Unreason.* Cambridge, Mass.: Harvard Business School Press, 1989.

Heider, John. *The Tao of Leadership: Leadership Strategies for a New Age.* New York: Bantam Books, 1985.

Helgesen, Sally. *The Female Advantage: Women's Ways of Leadership.* New York: Doubleday Currency, 1990.

Hibino, Shozo and Gerald Nadler. *Breakthrough Thinking*. Rocklin, Calif.: Prima Publishing, 1990.

Kotter, John P. "What Leaders Really Do," *Harvard Business Review*, May-June 1990.

Kuhn, Robert L., ed. *Handbook for Creative and Innovative Managers*. New York: McGraw-Hill, 1988.

Kushner, Malcolm. *The Light Touch: How to Use Humor for Business Success*. New York: Simon & Schuster, 1990.

Linden, Russell M. *From Vision to Reality: Strategies of Successful Innovators in Government*. Charlottesville, Va.: LEL Enterprises, 1990.

Lynch, Peter. *One Up on Wall Street*. New York: Penguin Books, 1989.

Neirenberg, Gerard I. *The Art of Creative Thinking*. New York: Simon & Schuster, 1982.

Nirenberg, Jesse S. *How to Sell Your Ideas*. New York: McGraw-Hill, 1984.

Norins, Hanley. *The Young & Rubicam Traveling Creative Workshop*. Englewood Cliffs, N.J.: Prentice-Hall, 1990.

Perry, William E. "Managers Can Unlearn the 'No' Response," *Computer News*.

Peters, Tom. *Thriving on Chaos: Handbook for a Management Revolution*. New York: Alfred A. Knopf, 1987.

Rico, Gabrielle Lusser. *Writing the Natural Way*. Los Angeles: J. P. Tarcher, 1983.

Robert, Michel and Alan Weiss. *The Innovation Formula: How Organizations Turn Change into Opportunity*. Cambridge, Mass.: Ballinger Publishing, 1988.

Rosenfield, Israel. *The Invention of Memory: A New View of the Brain*. New York: Basic Books, 1988.

Schrage, Michael. *Shared Minds: The New Technologies of Collaboration*. New York: Random House, 1990.

Schwartz, Peter. *The Art of the Long View*. New York: Doubleday, 1991.

Senge, Peter M. *The Fifth Discipline: The Art and Practice of the Learning Organization*. New York: Doubleday Currency, 1990.

Taylor, Anne P. *School Zone*. Corrales, N. Mex.: School Zone, Inc., 1983.

Tichy, Noel and Ram Charan. "Speed, Simplicity, Self-Confidence: An Interview with Jack Welch," *Harvard Business Review*, September–October 1989.

von Oech, Roger. *A Kick in the Seat of the Pants: Using Your Explorer, Artist, Judge and Warrior to Be More Creative*. New York: Harper & Row, 1986.

_____. *A Whack on the Side of the Head*. Menlo Park, Calif.: Creative Think, 1983.

Wurman, Richard Saul. *Information Anxiety*. New York: Doubleday, 1989.

Wycoff, Joyce. *Mindmapping: Your Personal Guide to Exploring Creativity and Problem-Solving*. New York: Berkley Books, 1991.

Yasuda, Yuzo. *40 Years, 20 Million Suggestions: The Toyota Suggestion System*. Cambridge, Mass.: Productivity Press, 1991.

Wanted

Dead or Alive:

"KILLER" PHRASES

We are collecting Killer Phrases from around the world to include in our next edition of *What a Great Idea!* Please send us your phrases, and if we use one in the book . . . we'll credit you for having contributed it and we'll send you a free copy of our full-color, 11" x 17" Killer Phrase poster, suitable for framing and displaying on your conference room or office wall.*

Collect the Killer Phrases used in your office, in your home, and at your school. Make it a team or a family effort.

Send your Killer Phrases to: **Killer Phrases**, c/o Creative Management Group, Queen Charlotte Square, 226 East High Street, Charlottesville, VA 22901–5177 USA.

*To obtain a Killer Phrase poster, simply mail your request to Creative Management Group at the above address and enclose $2.50 for postage and handling.

Share Your Great Ideas!

We want to include your great ideas in our next edition of *What a Great Idea!* We will provide a free subscription to our newsletter, *Creativity Today*, to everyone who submits ideas. We are interested in your ideas concerning:

- Running meetings
- Brainstorming techniques
- Cutting out junk work
- Communicating your vision
- Generating publicity
- New uses for Idea Mapping
- Speeding up your operations
- Self-directed work teams

My great idea is:

_____

_____

_____

_____

Send your great ideas to: **Great Ideas**, c/o Creative Management Group, 226 East High Street, Charlottesville, VA 22901–5177 USA.

Baking Soda Champs

Following are the participants from Hewlett-Packard who set the record for suggesting the most uses for baking soda—eighty-three uses in three minutes. Congratulations to: Dale Abbott, Bill Anderson, Dave Arndt, Melisa Atkeson, Diane Bange, Pat Ciccarone, Mary Connaughton, Cynthia Cotetta, Russ Dodd, Terry Dombrowski, Laurie Eldridge, Melissa Elgin, Joyce Eyler, Tom Furlong, Kevin Gilroy, Jeff Glick, Lee Gravatte, John Guy, Marge Harmon, Melissa Hatala, Mark Kanefsky, Murray Kaplan, Jerry Kolb, Debbie Langdon, Cabella Langsam, Mike Larson, Mark Lewis, Dan Marino, Carrie Maslen, Anne Mason, Hugh McNelis, Tom Meringolo, Rich O'Donnell, Todd Palmer, Peter Romness, Dave Saba, Susan Sabo, Susan Simpson, Carol Sommers, Marty Stenson, Gloria Summers, Don Swartz, Gus Takacs, Skip Trahern, Becky Vogt, Mike Watanabe, Ray Weber, Jan Wernecker, Steve Young, Tom Young.